C000154304

THE LIFE OF
BRIAN HONOUR

THE LIFE OF BRIAN HONOUR

JOHN RIDDLE

Foreword by Peter Beardsley

APEX PUBLISHING LTD

First published in 2008 by

Apex Publishing Ltd

PO Box 7086, Clacton on Sea, Essex, CO15 5WN

www.apexpublishing.co.uk

Copyright © 2008 by John Riddle
The author has asserted his moral rights

British Library Cataloguing-in-Publication Data
A catalogue record for this book
is available from the British Library

ISBN 1-906358-22-2   978-1-906358-22-8

All rights reserved. This book is sold subject to the condition, that no part of this book is to be reproduced, in any shape or form. Or by way of trade, stored in a retrieval system or transmitted in any form or by any means, electronic, mechanical, photocopying, recording, be lent, re-sold, hired out or otherwise circulated in any form of binding or cover other than that in which it is published and without a similar condition, including this condition being imposed on the subsequent purchaser, without prior permission of the copyright holder.

Typeset in 12pt Times New Roman

Production Manager: Chris Cowlin

Cover Design: Siobhan Smith

Printed and bound in Great Britain
By Biddles Ltd., Kings Lynn

Acknowledgements

I would like to thank everyone, including the following people, for their assistance, help and support in producing *The Life of Brian Honour*:

My partner, Lorna Young; the staff of the Central Library in Hartlepool; Tottenham Hotspur; the Honour family of Horden; Bishop Auckland FC; Bernie Slaven; members of the 'Into the Blue' supporters website; the 'Into the Mad Crowd' website; the *Hartlepool Mail*; Gareth Healy; Bob Moncur; vital.hartlepool@hotmail.co.uk; Bernie Slaven; Tommy Miller; Joe Allon; Hartlepool Athletic; Peter Beardsley; Joan Zettle; Krimo; neil.brown.newcastle fans.com; the Poolie Bunker website; www.stato.com; Hartlepool Sunday League; and the many long-suffering fans of Hartlepool United, who have made this small tribute to Brian possible.

Contents

Foreword

It is an honour to do this foreword for Brian's book.

In the twilight of my career I had the pleasure of working with Brian when he was a coach at Hartlepool United.

Brian was helpful and treated me like a 'king'.

He once said to me, "I would walk on broken glass for you, Pedro."

Brian Honour was a different class of person, never mind a different class of footballer.

I hope you will enjoy reading his remarkable life story as much as I did.

Peter Beardsley

Introduction

I remember when I wrote my first essay, at Jesmond Road Junior School in Hartlepool, under the watchful eye of my teacher, Mr Alan Tozer JP, and the comments he added alongside the average mark - "Must do better".

Over the next 50 years I carried those three words with me as a spur to doing just that - doing things better.

When I realised my ambition to become a journalist, an ambition that was to take slightly longer than Brian Honour's dream to become a professional footballer, I still had those words firmly planted in my mind.

At *The Paper*, an English language newspaper published in the Canary Islands, where by that time I was living following my retirement from the Probation Service, I met Sandie Laming-Powell.

Sandie was a professional journalist, having worked for the *News of the World* as its fashion editor. Alas she didn't teach me a great deal about fashion, as my dress sense bears testament, but each week we battled to make the next edition better than the last.

I think I am a better writer thanks to Sandie.

I have to admit that I am no Andrew Morton, nor is Brian Honour as famous outside Hartlepool as Morton's most distinguished subject, the late Diana, Princess of Wales. But I have tried to adhere to the same principles by selecting what areas of Brian's life to include, which ones to highlight and which events to omit.

If you are on a sunny beach somewhere warm or in front

of a roaring log fire and doze off while reading *The Life of Brian*, that's another sentence I can add to my CV - "I cured someone's insomnia". By the same token, if you are an avid reader and plough through these pages cover to cover only stopping for a coffee or toilet break, well that too is an achievement in my eyes. However, if you flick through the pages and replace it on the library shelf to gather dust or if you are a member of the journalistic brotherhood and review this book and savage its contents, well that too will help - it will send me back to the drawing board to follow Alan Tozer's advice - "Must do better".

But this book is not about me. It's a frank, sometimes sad, often revealing account about Brian Honour, a diminutive lad from a pit village who had an ambition to become a professional footballer.

Our diverse lives would converge many years later when we both had achieved our respective dreams. Our common interest in sport and football in particular, and the love of a 'Cinderella' club in the north-east of England - Hartlepool United - would unite us to write this account of *The Life of Brian*.

John Riddle

Legend

The word 'legend' means many things to many people.

The *Oxford English Dictionary* defines the word as 'a traditional story or myth'.

Go to bonnie Scotland and the word is synonymous with a monster that apparently lurks beneath Loch Ness. Travel to Nottingham and you will hear tales of Robin Hood and his band of outlaws. Even as far away as the mountain regions of Nepal, mention the word and the locals will speak of 'big-footed' beasts that lurch across the snow-covered peaks.

However, if you find yourself in Victoria Park, home of Hartlepool United Football Club, on the north-east coast of England, the word 'legend' can be defined in two words - Brian Honour.

Brian was one of five boys born to Sheila and John Honour in the former mining village of Horden in County Durham. The five boys all wanted to play football from a very early age and the 'Honour Boys' graced the fields of West Bromwich Albion, Oldham, Newcastle United, Workington, Middlesbrough and Hartlepool United as well as the non-League circuit. They were truly a footballing family; not as famous as the Charltons, but certainly bigger!

Brian Honour was born on 16th February 1964. His earliest recollections of his dad, the late John, were of a man "who walked with a stick". John Honour, like so many men at the time, worked for the National Coal Board at Horden Colliery where he had an horrific accident underground. From that day until his death, his walking stick was a constant companion. Brian's dad died in 1971 as a result of his injuries at the age of just 49 years. Brian Honour was only seven years old at the time of his father's untimely death.

Brian's mam, Sheila, then had the responsibility of looking

after her five growing sons - Raymond, Allen, John, Billy and little Brian - alone. She spent the rest of her life looking after 'her boys', initially at the family home in Twelfth Street, Horden. The majority of the streets were named simply First Street, Second Street, and so on. They were two-up two-down back-to-backs with what today would seem to be primitive facilities, some still having outside toilets and no bath.

However, this was a rock-solid Labour community whose whole life and existence centred around 'the pit', as Horden Colliery was known. Manny Shinwell, later to become Lord Manny, was the local MP.

A year before Brian started school, the family received a visitor to their modest home, which at this time was 26 Warren Street, Horden. Brian takes up the story.

"This man, a famous man from Port Vale, came to try and sign my elder brother John. The man brought my mam and dad a bone china tea set and gave us four lads a china mug each. I remember him patting me on the head and asking my name. He give me a signed copy of his photograph. The man wrote, 'to my little pal Brian' and signed it," explained Brian.

And the man? Well, it was none other than Stan Matthews, probably the greatest winger ever produced by England and later to be knighted by Her Majesty the Queen. Matthews was a legend, but he had to wait until 1953, the year of the Coronation, to win the medal he most wanted - the FA Cup - in that thrilling 4-3 final in which Blackpool came from 3-1 down to win.

At four years of age Brian Honour had met his first legend.

These were the days when any football scout could go to a local pit and shout down the shaft that he was looking for a big centre half. The cage would come up from the bottom of the pit and three or four lads would emerge, all black, with coal dust, ready to play.

The north-east of England has always produced a plethora of fine footballers, including 'Wor Jackie' Milburn, Jack and Bobby Charlton, Bryan Robson and, in little Horden Colliery, the Honours.

Brian would always look forward to his brother John coming home from West Bromwich because it was always like Christmas. Brian would travel with his uncle John or brother Allen in a blue mini to Durham Railway Station to meet John, who had travelled from Birmingham New Street. Brian was always the first in the car because he knew John would be bringing some goodies. Sometimes it would be a Baggies strip, pennant or rosettes, but the most memorable gift was an autograph book. John had kept a book containing the signatures of the members of all the big teams - Manchester United and the like - who had visited. John had got all the players from the top flight to sign the book and at the end of one season that was little Brian's gift.

He loved John coming home from West Brom; he just loved it.

Brian Honour started school at Sunderland Road Juniors, known locally as 'the old tin school'. It has long since disappeared, along with the mines in the area, but Brian remembers his first days at school with affection, and he describes Mr Peter Dunn, his old headmaster, as being "football mad". Another teacher who took an interest in our diminutive fledgling soccer star was Mr Anderson.

Brian's brother John had also been through the school and he went on to play with West Bromwich Albion. The teachers at the school were convinced that they would find another Horden lad to grace the football league. And they were not wrong!

However, the old school was eventually demolished and Brian and his classmates moved to Cotsford Primary School in Horden. The headteacher there was again Mr Dunn, whom Brian describes as "a bit of a disciplinarian". He thinks his retired head may now live in the local seaside resort of Crimdon. Brian knows that Mr Dunn's daughter teaches in the area, following in her father's footsteps.

At Cotsford Junior School, Brian was part of the team that reached the Echo/Mail Cup final in 1974, losing out to Edenhall. Brian reluctantly accepted defeat and a losers' medal. The presenter of this first award was actually his brother John, who had been invited to hand out the prizes that day. Brian's school were League champions but missed out on a League and Cup double.

He then played in a representative match between Peterlee and District Boys and Hartlepool Boys and, although reports say he was a midfielder with potential, Peterlee lost 5-1. In the Hartlepool Boys team that day was an outstanding player at number 5 - John Borthwick - and a lad called Linighan. Both would later become Brian's teammates at Hartlepool United, and the latter would score the winning goal for Arsenal in the FA Cup Final!

The following season in the Echo/Mail Cup final Cotsford Juniors would meet the cup holders Peterlee Edenhall, and this time the result would be so very different.

More than 400 turned out to watch the game at North Blunts Ground, Peterlee. Brian scored a goal and his team won 5-2 to add the Cup to the League Championship and the George Wilson Cup for a remarkable treble. Young Honour also received the Man of the Match shield for his performance in the Cup final. It would not be the last Man of the Match award he would receive during his long career.

In the summer of 1977, 13-year-old Brian Honour received yet another award as Boy of the Week at Butlins Holiday Camp, Filey. The coaching week sponsored by the *Daily Express* and Sir Billy Butlins Holiday Camp saw Brian head and shoulders above the rest. He was presented with his award by Clive Clark, the former West Brom and England player, and received a free week's holiday.

Clive had been born in Leeds and went on to play for United, QPR, Preston North End and West Brom. It was for the Baggies that he appeared in the 1967 League Cup final, scoring twice against QPR but still ending up on the losing side. Rodney Marsh scored for QPR, supported by Mark Lazarus and Roger Morgan. But Clive did add a winners' medal to his collection when Preston North End were promoted as champions of the Third Division in 1970-71.

So Brian Honour had met another legend - not as well known as Sir Stan, but nevertheless a true professional who graced Wembley Stadium before 98,000 fans.

When Brian left to go to the 'big school' to start his secondary education, he attended Horden Modern Boys School, where he was to stay for three years until 1978. Then the local council decided that, under some educational restructuring, the schools of neighbouring villages Horden and Blackhall should be combined to form Yoden Hall School.

Brian's first secondary school is now a primary school and Yoden Hall is a residential home for old footballers. Well, that's actually a bit of poetic licence, as the home is for the more mature villagers rather than solely for old footballers. Needless to say, there are plenty of old players kicking around County Durham.

Brian recently moved to a new private estate within striking distance of the old Yoden Hall School - the posh end of Blackhall these days!

It was at Yoden Hall that the fledgling talents of young Brian came to the attention of the school staff in the persons of Mr Mike Weetman and, strangely enough, a great local Rugby Union player, Bill Dale.

Bill Dale took an immediate shine to Brian. He was well aware that Brian's elder brother John had gone on to play in the Football League with West Bromwich Albion.

"Mr Dale was fantastic," explained Brian, "and my fitness levels went up a ton."

Bill Dale was a quality rugby player in his day, something of a man mountain. In later years, however, Bill would somewhat abandon the game played by men with odd-shaped balls to become a fervent Hartlepool United fan.

So what were Bill Dale's recollections of little Brian at Yoden Hall School more than 25 years ago?

I met Bill in the Cyril Knowles Stand at Hartlepool United during the half-time interval of a home game with Tranmere Rovers, and this is what he told me:

"Well, as I recall, little Brian wanted to take the corners, the throw-ins, the penalties and the goal kicks. He was, in a word, enthusiastic.

"He would come onto the field, shorts past his knees, socks rolled down and a runny nose, looking like a scruffy little urchin.

"But his talent was outrageous. Players around him played above themselves when Brian was on the pitch. He was an inspiration to everyone who played around him."

After the interval Bill and I settled down to watch the current Hartlepool United team beat Tranmere Rovers 3-1. It was a great night!

Brian was selected to play for East Durham Schools FA whilst at Yoden Hall, and in the typed programme of the day he is described as playing a major part in the team's success. It reports that he had signed Associate Schoolboy forms with Aston Villa. Also on the team were Ian Cranson, who had trials at Ipswich Town; Keith Oakley, also on Schoolboys forms with Villa; and Gary Renwick and David Hall, who were both scheduled for trials at Ipswich. So there was quite an array of budding talent.

In the English Schools Last 32, the East Durham Schools FA beat the Carlisle Under-15s 2-0 to progress to the next round, at which stage they would go out to Bradford Boys 1-0.

Before Brian left school he had to go on work experience. His classmates chose to spend time with the Army, in factories or in garages, but Brian chose to clean football boots at Aston Villa. That gave him some insight into the role of an apprentice footballer and Brian, for his efforts, received a new pair of football boots and a Villa shirt - small size, naturally.

Brian Honour graduated from Yoden Hall without 'honours', although he does himself a little injustice when he laughingly says, "To be honest, I was as thick as a chop," as he did secure GCSEs in English, Art, Geography and Mathematics.

The geography qualification came in quite handy for Brian as he travelled between the collieries, Darlington and Hartlepool, and also in later life when he found himself at Spennymoor, Durham City, Peterlee and Bishop Auckland.

He's a pretty good artist off the field as well as on it, and some of his illustrations are worthy of an exhibition.

It was whilst at Yoden Hall, encouraged by Bill Dale and the other teachers at the school, that Brian attracted the attention of football scouts. In those days the scouts would regularly travel north to watch East Durham Schoolboys, Chester le Street Boys Club and clubs on Tyneside, which would eventually produce the likes of Steve Bruce, Bryan Robson and, of course, the incomparable Gazza.

Brian was selected to play for East Durham Boys, which was quite an honour for any lad, as the club had produced Brian Little, who went on to play for Aston Villa; Brian's brother John, who made the grade at West Bromwich Albion and Pools; and Ian Cranson, who plied his trade at Portman Road with Ipswich Town.

The Villa scout, George Walker, spotted the early potential of Brian Honour and at 13 years of age, in 1977, the little lad from Horden and Blackhall was invited to Villa Park.

Over the next three years, after signing Schoolboy forms under the watchful eye of Ron Saunders, the then Villa manager, Brian travelled 'down south' to train and play as often as he could.

Brian recalls his first day: "I was introduced to Mr Saunders and then to the star of Aston Villa at the time, Brian Little. He was one of my heroes from this area. I was a bit gobsmacked at the time."

Brian Little was great and told the young lad, "You will like it here, it's a great set-up."

Brian Honour loved Villa and thought he was all set to sign on as an apprentice for the Midland giants, who would go on to win the European Cup in 1982. He had three years with them as a Schoolboy and had obviously impressed everyone. They had another local hero in Little and Brian Honour would not have been the first lad from Hartlepool United to be associated with the European Cup. John McGovern lifted the famous trophy in 1979 and again the following year. If one lad who played rugby at Henry Smith's could do it - well, why not a lad from Horden who had kicked a ball ever since the day he could walk?

The three years at Villa, although they prepared Brian Honour for a career that would span more than two decades, did not prepare him at all for the disappointments he would face.

Gutted!

Another lad from the area, Keith Oakley, the son of former Hartlepool United goalie Norman Oakley, was also at Villa. Both lads were about to leave school and Brian was out training every day to keep his fitness up. Brian knew that, because of his size, he was never going to be a 'big lad', and so his speed and skill would have to compensate for his lack of inches.

Keith Oakley had received a letter from Villa saying that they would not be continuing their interest, and Keith would subsequently disappear into the non-League game as do so many other wannabe professionals. It's not to their detriment, it's just part of life in the beautiful game.

Brian, on the other hand, had not received such a letter and so, thinking that no news was good news, he went out running. However, when he had completed his regulation five miles for the day he returned home to see his mother standing on the doorstep clutching a letter.

His heart sank to his boots.

Those last few yards down Twelfth Street, Horden, he recalls, seemed like 12 miles. His heart was pounding and he was sweating buckets. He knew what was coming.

The letter, once opened, revealed his worst fears: Aston Villa had rejected him because "he was too small".

Brian Honour was gutted.

He was faced with leaving school with no job lined up. What was he to do? His four GCSEs would not get him far.

All the lads at school were going down the pit - the same Horden Colliery that had crippled Brian's father John and had led to his premature death.

Fate, once again, had dealt Brian a crap hand.

He had lost his father at the age of six and now, on the

threshold of what he thought would be a career in football, he felt rejection again.

So size really does matter, he thought.

Brian Honour may well have cried himself to sleep that night, as his dream of gracing Villa Park had suddenly been plunged into darkness - the darkness that was Horden Colliery.

A Silver Lining?

The next morning, however, Brian bounced back.

He was reassured by his big brother Allen, who was more like a father, and his loving mother, and things did not look too bad as the sun shone through the window of the house in Twelfth Street.

Brian vowed, "I will show them they are wrong."

His dear mother responded with a smile, "Yes, there's many a good thing in a little parcel."

Brian particularly remembers her smile. On occasions that was the only thing that kept him going; that and the determination to be a professional footballer.

So 1980 may well have been a good year for Brian Clough and Nottingham Forest who won the European Cup, but it was not too good a year for 'our Brian'.

So off he went to the pit office to get the application form to join the National Coal Board and enter the black hole that was Horden Colliery. It was the only place to go.

I will have no problem being small there, he thought as he went to the pit head office. But he discovered there were four lads chasing every vacancy.

On the way back from the pit Brian picked up a copy of the *Northern Echo*, the morning newspaper for the Durham area, as opposed to the *Hartlepool Mail*, which came out in the evening.

Would there be any other jobs? Did he really have to go down the pit? Many thoughts were buzzing round in his head.

When he got home and settled down in front of the warm coal fire with a pot of tea from his ma, Brian started to read the *Echo*.

In it he spotted an article that would literally change his life. Darlington Football Club would be holding trials at

Feethams over the Bank Holiday weekend and anybody interested was invited to apply.

Using all his skills from his English GCSE and a little help from his mam, Brian penned a letter and hurried to the post office as soon as he had finished it to post it off to the Quakers.

"I was not going to build my hopes up again, but I still wanted to play football," he explained.

Following that chance buying of the *Northern Echo*, a well-written letter and with his fingers crossed for good luck, Brian waited ... and waited.

Eventually the reply came: could he present himself at Feethams for a couple of days?

Yes he could!

On the appointed day, Brian travelled from Horden to Darlington by bus, which in those days took ages. When he arrived in Darlington he discovered that the trials were not being played on the pitch at Feethams but on South Park, an area behind one of the stands where goals had simply been marked out with cones.

It was chaos. More than 100 lads had turned up for the trials.

How would Brian, who already had an inferiority complex about his size, stand out?

He could only do his best.

Brian had been playing with a group of lads for about 20 minutes when came the dreaded tap on the shoulder. His immediate thought was: that's it, I'm off home, rejected by even bloody Darlington.

The man standing behind him, whom he now knows was Kenny Ellis, an ex-pro on the coaching staff at Feethams, said to him, "Follow me, son."

His heart was in his mouth again.

He trotted behind Mr Ellis, thinking that he would be given his bus fare home and have to face disappointment yet again. Brian recollects:

"Kenny took me into the manager's office and there sat Jimmy Shoulder, the first team coach, a former Hartlepool United player. Next to him was Billy Elliot, who had been at

Sunderland and later Bishop Auckland. Bishops had won the Amateur Cup on no fewer than ten occasions, so Billy and Jimmy had a great knowledge of the game. Jimmy Shoulder had also managed the Australian national team."

"Come in, son. Sit down," said Jimmy, and he introduced Brian to Billy Elliot.

"You did alright out there today," he smiled.

Brian just nodded. For once he was lost for words, which in later years would astonish some referees!

The Darlington management team then offered Brian a two-year apprenticeship.

"I was gobsmacked. All I had ever wanted to do was play football," explained Brian.

However, he did not sign there and then. He was asked to go home and talk to his family about the proposed deal. After talking to his man and elder brother Allen, who had assumed the role of father figure after Brian's dad had passed away and bought him his first pair of football boots, they decided they would go to Darlington for the next home game, as guests of the club.

Darlington were playing Newport County, who subsequently lost their League status and these days ply their trade in the Conference South Division, visiting such exotic teams as Bognor Regis and Bath.

During the meeting with the Darlington management team, Brian, his mam, but mainly his elder brother Allen asked all the appropriate questions about such things as the travelling arrangements and his board and lodgings. Would he have to live in Darlington?

That thought still makes Brian squirm today. Live in Darlington? Never!

At the conclusion of the discussions Brian Honour became a Darlington player on a two-year apprenticeship, starting on 18th August 1980. He was paid £16 per week plus £10 towards his travel and £10 towards his board and lodgings.

He never did find digs in Darlington, but he gave the Quakers quite a few many years later when he transferred to

Hartlepool United.

In the next season Brian, aged 17 years, was still on the small side. Well come on, be honest! Brian has always been on the small side except when it comes to the size of his heart.

His wages had increased to £20 by 1981 and then, as his apprenticeship came to an end, he faced a nervous few weeks again as he waited to be called to the manager's office.

A letter arrived for Brian. Oh no, he thought, not another letter.

However, this time he need not have worried!

The letter, dated 26th October 1981, was from Ted Croker, the Secretary of the Football Association, inviting Brian to Lilleshall that November. It contained the names of the other students taking part, including Andy McAvoy (Blackpool), Nick Pickering (Sunderland), David Seaman (Leeds United), Trevor Steven (Burnley), Barry Venison (Sunderland) plus, of course, the recipient of the letter - Brian Honour (Darlington).

Seaman, as we all know, would become a legend at Arsenal with 400 appearances and he would keep goal for England on 75 occasions. Venison would have a distinguished career with Sunderland, Liverpool and Newcastle and win two England caps. Trevor Steven would move to Everton and appear for the Toffees 210 times and pick up 36 England caps, and Nick Pickering would also win an England cap, his finest hour being at the 1987 FA Cup final. Coventry had beaten Manchester United on the way to the final and faced Tottenham at Wembley before a crowd of 98,000. As history reveals, Coventry won 3-2 with a diving header from Keith Houchen, who had also worn the famous shirt of Hartlepool United.

Yes, Brian was in legendary company in October 1981.

Soon after Brian had signed for the Quakers he was contacted by Dave Richardson, one of the youth team coaches at Villa. Dave had moved to Filbert Street and he told Brian that if he was still interested in an apprenticeship the door was open to join Leicester City. Brian, having already signed for Darlington, was a man of his word even in those days and politely declined.

Dave Richardson, in return, accepted that he was dealing with a young man of honour.

First Professional Contract

On his 18th birthday in 1982 Brian Honour achieved his life ambition - he signed a professional contract, his first ever, with Darlington Football Club. Initially that contract was for just 12 months, but on £60 a week plus appearance money and a bonus, he felt at long last he had arrived. The disappointment of Aston Villa was put to rest - a least for the time being.

Brian used to practise his footballing skills on the gable end of the houses in Twelfth Street. Quite often a neighbour of his, Janet Hall, would walk past on her way home from school, carrying washing from the launderette where her mother worked, and young Brian used to try to knock the bag of washing out of her hand. Horrible little boy!

Over the years, however, Janet, who lived at number 23 Twelfth Street, and Brian, who lived at number 49, became mates and they would sometimes walk home from school together. Using her for target practice soon stopped, a good friendship developed and in 1982, at the time that he got his first pro contract, they started courting.

On 8th July 1984, Janet's 18th birthday, with another contract under his belt, Brian bought Janet a ring and they became engaged.

This is the grass-roots end of football, Mr Rooney: players on £60 a week, a ring from H.J. Samuels and selling the wedding photograph rights to the *Hartlepool Mail* and not *Hello* magazine. That was the reality of the scenario.

The honeymoon period for Brian and Janet continued and they would remain forever friends. They have now been married 21 years and are looking forward to their silver wedding, grandchildren and everything else associated with a long and happy union.

The Early Days at Feethams

Brian played for Darlington in the first round of the Northern Intermediate Cup against Leeds United at Feethams in 1980. Billy Elliot refused to allow the match to go to penalties after two draws and felt the lads deserved a taste of the big time at Elland Road. The manager went on, "I was delighted with the performance. It's the best set of youngsters we have had here for years."

Darlington were inspired by little Brian Honour and, had it not been for a reflex save from Leeds goalkeeper Seaman, he would have scored.

Andy Brown, writing in the local paper, says, "Stell and Honour dominated midfield but Quakers forwards could make little headway against a powerful Leeds defence."

Several hundred fans cheered off both sides at the end of an entertaining game.

In those days Brian Honour was the nominated penalty taker. He slotted home spot kicks as Darlington Youth team crashed 4-1 to Lincoln and again in the away win at Ferryhill Athletic.

Brian played his initial game for the first team in a friendly against Sunderland. They should have taken notice that day, as little Honour would come back to haunt the Black Cats some years later.

As teenage skipper of the juniors, Brian got a taste of the big time. He displayed some fine skills and confirmed that he was now ready to challenge for a regular midfield spot. Fred Barber, a Darlington team mate, and Brian also went to the England training camp together.

Brian's League debut was set for the home game against Crewe Alexandra after the pitch had been cleared on snow.

Darlington were in the same boat as many lower League

clubs in 1982. They were £95,000 in debt and asked the public to help. A subsequent appeal raised more than £50,000 and set the club back on the road to recovery.

In the meantime, Brian and some of the other young lads successfully completed a course at New College, Durham, run by course co-ordinator Mr John Hayes, who explained, "The course is for 16 to 19 year olds and one of the aims is to prepare them for adult life. They will set up homes at some time, face things like burst pipes and perhaps buy items on hire purchase."

One of the other apprentices, Scott Duncan, 19, from Gosforth, who had been at Darlington for two years, proffered a realistic appraisal of life at the lower end of the Football League pyramid: "Football is a dodgy game and if management said we are not good enough at least we would now have something to help us in later life."

Prophetic words indeed from Scott, and they would come back to haunt Brian Honour not so very far down the apprenticeship path.

Darlington boss, Billy Elliot, acknowledged that less than one in five of the apprentices would make the grade and he would encourage all of them to take as many courses as they could.

In the 1982-83 season Brian Honour finally made the first team photocall and is pictured sitting next to his manager with coach George Herd in the second row. Brian would work with George Herd on another occasion.

Brian's first full game for Darlington was in the Milk Cup second leg at Peterborough. Significantly, when he moved to Hartlepool United, he would make his League debut for Pools against Peterborough, this time at the Victoria Ground.

Brian's next away day was to Essex and a match with promotion favourites Colchester United. United went ahead after 15 minutes with a goal from Allison and that was the score at half-time. Alan Walsh scored the first of his two goals after the break. Brian Honour raced through on the right and crossed into the penalty area where the striker was waiting to tap the ball in from close range.

How many times in his career would Honour do that?

The score on the night ended 2-2 and Honour was Darlington's Man of the Match with a rating of 8/10 in the local press.

Honour was again Man of the Match when the Crazy Gang from Wimbledon visited Feethams. The smallest crowd of the season - just over 1,100 - saw Darlington waste chances, although Brian was denied a goal by a super save from Dave Beasant. The final score was a 2-0 win to Wimbledon.

Honour was also Man of the Match in the Crewe game and in the 3-2 win over Chester City when Brian scored. Super sub Honour grabbed the winner five minutes from time when he crashed the ball home.

Darlington eased their relegation worries with another 2-0 win over Northampton Town with Brian scoring again.

Brian's games for Darlington had attracted rave reviews from sports reporters, but when Billy Elliot was sacked Brian's future with the Quakers was suddenly under threat.

Nice One Cyril

Brian's honeymoon period with Darlington was soon to come to an abrupt end. Cyril Knowles was appointed manager after a successful career with Tottenham Hotspur and England had come to an end.

Cyril played 39 games for Middlesbrough before being signed by Bill Nicholson at Spurs. He would make more than 400 appearances in a wonderful career that attracted four England caps, three more than his boss Nicholson. Cyril would have attracted more international honours had it not been for the outstanding form of Leeds United's Terry Cooper.

Although Brian Honour was on the team photograph for the 1983-84 season, his days were numbered.

However, he did manage a few games. In the first leg of the Milk Cup at Halifax Town, Brian slotted home a goal to give the Quakers a narrow lead to take back to Feethams. He was Man of the Match in a few more games, including the FA Cup second round 2-0 victory at Altringham. In the Associate Members Cup at Mansfield, Brian scored twice when Darlington beat the home side 3-1. Journalist John Dean awarded the Honour Man of the Match with a mark of 9/10.

Cyril Knowles, however, was a member of the old school who seemed to think that to be a good professional you needed to be at least 6 foot and over 12 stones and with the speed of Shergar.

Brian may well have been able to keep up with the famous racehorse in his prime, but he was never going to be 6 foot or weigh more than 11 stone, even when he reached retirement.

Big Cyril pulled no punches. He told Brian, "I am going to have to let you go. I want big strong lads and you are just too small."

The sentiments from Aston Villa had come back to haunt Brian, and he realised that it was no good arguing with Mr Knowles.

Had Cyril Knowles' opinion been accepted as universal, then around the grounds of England and Scotland we might never have seen such players as Billy Bremner (5 foot 5), Jimmy 'Jinky' Johnstone (5 foot 4) and the comparative giant Johnny Giles (5 foot 7) all of whom were vertically challenged, but proved the critics wrong. Bremner was rejected by both Arsenal and Chelsea for being too small but, as we all know, his career took off at both Leeds United and Scotland. 'Jinky' went on to become a legend in his own lifetime at Celtic. And Johnny Giles played for Leeds United almost 400 times to add to his 100 for Manchester United and, with 59 caps for the Republic of Ireland, he was also a legend. All three players received international recognition.

But not so for Brian. He was demoralised.

In the summer of 1984, having just become engaged to be married on the back of what Brian and Janet thought was a promising career with Darlington, their dream was shattered. Brian was out of work and on the dole, a single lad living at home back in Horden with his widowed mother, and his wedding plans were put on hold.

Brian was certainly not in the mood for singing 'Nice One Cyril'.

In the village all talk focused on the National Union of Mineworkers headed by Arthur Scargill, who was taking on Prime Minister Maggie Thatcher. The starting point of the dispute was more than 100 miles away in Barnsley, where the NCB had announced it was closing Cortonwood Colliery.

It was a strike that would divide communities, set brother against brother, father against son and eventually lead to the demise of the coal industry.

Brian has never been political. He did not go with his mates, the miners, to the picket line, but instead gave what financial help he could to support the fight against the Tory government. It wasn't much.

There wasn't a picket line most days at Horden because it is was a 'wet pit' and essential staff had to go underground to keep the pumps working. Everyone hoped that when the Government had been defeated and the miners strike was over, jobs would once again be available. When the men walked out on 5th March 1984, little did the miners realise that it would be more than a year before they would return. These were hard times for the miners, really hard times.

There had been strikes before, but in 1984 the miners' union led by Arthur Scargill dug in for a lengthy and bitter battle. In the end, however, the biggest losers were the miners and their families. Typically the pit villages of Horden, Blackhall and Easington bore the brunt in County Durham.

The 1974 miners strike had brought down the Edward Heath Government, but five years into her reign as Prime Minister, Mrs Thatcher, the 'Iron Lady' was not going to lose. She had made sure that the power stations had stockpiled coal. This time she said the miners were not going to hold the country to ransom. The lady may not have been for turning, but she had certainly planned to make sure she held most of the cards. The deck was stacked in her favour and she made the miners and their families suffer.

Soup kitchens were set up in Brian's home village and many pubs in mining areas allowed miners credit until they themselves were forced to close. Butchers, grocers and other business did the same.

It was hard, but Scargill was as hard as the Yorkshire coal he once mined. In a ballot the union had voted that, unless a colliery was closed on the grounds that the coal was exhausted, they would strike. The National Executive tried to get a debate going to overturn the 1981 resolution, but Arthur Scargill overruled the motion.

Pickets were dispatched to collieries all around the country to ask men to stay away from work and support the strike. Nottingham was a particular target for Scargill's Yorkshire colleagues, but in the north in Durham it divided communities and in some cases entire families.

An old Tory ploy was working - divide and rule.

Police were drafted in to maintain order. In some mining areas, young men had chosen to join the police force or the Army rather than go down the pit. They were thus forced to face their brothers who had gone down the pit across the picket line. Some families even 20 years later remain divided. It was a bitter, bitter struggle.

Confrontation, soup kitchens, families going cold and no end in sight was the scenario our young professional Brian faced.

Maggie Thatcher may have put thousands of Yorkshire miners and their colleagues in the Durham coalfield out of work, but it was a Yorkshireman in the form of Cyril Knowles that had pushed Brian onto the dole queue.

Lesser men might have hung up their boots right there are then. But I think it was another Tory leader, Winston Churchill, who once said, "It's not the size of the dog in the fight; it's the size of the fight in the dog." Brian Honour may have only stood at five feet seven inches, but this little chunk of Horden granite had the tenacity of a pit bull terrier and the resolve to match.

They say revenge is a dish best served cold, and it would be five long years before Brian would have an opportunity to test that theory. But when he did, it would be a sweet, sweet taste.

The Summer of Discontent

During that summer, as the battle of Orgreave Colliery hit the headlines, Brian secured no work. However, he was offered a place at Peterlee Newtown playing for pleasure rather than pounds. Peterlee in those days played in a strip not unlike that of Maradona's Argentina, but there the similarity ended.

Brian had friends there in Terry Bainbridge, who had played for Hartlepool United, Barry Corfield and 'Steppy' Johnson, who was later to make a fair packet with a coach company. He had no money left to jingle in his pocket out of the £27 a week dole money, just like his mates, and there was no coal for the fire at his mam's house. If he wanted a hot shower he had to go to the pit-head baths. But at least, come August, he was playing football again.

So the miners' strike hit our little striker as well as the entire mining community. And, as summer 1984 turned to autumn, the financial hardship was biting hard throughout County Durham.

Brian and Janet's plans for a wedding were still on hold. Janet's father, Derek Hall, was a miner and so putting food on the table was his prime concern. Providing a flash wedding for his lovely daughter would have to wait, but he would do it one day.

Men who had been amongst the best paid manual workers in the country had been without wages for more than six months by this time. With their savings exhausted and just a few pounds from the union, these were very hard times for Horden men and their mining colleagues. Many families relied on the food parcels and soup kitchens, and the women of the pit villages rallied as they had done in 1939-45 to keep their pride and food in the kids' bellies.

In September the Coal Board offered the miners a deal, but Scargill refused it. A number of strikers returned to work, which raised the temperature of the strike and violence erupted on the picket lines. In one incident, a South Wales taxi driver lost his life when a building block was dropped on his car for taking 'scab' labour to the pit.

After Christmas 1984, which was one of the most miserable on record for anyone living in a pit village, the trickle became a flood in many areas.

On 3rd March, the union summoned more than 200 delegates to a special NUM conference. A bitter and heated debate ensued and it is alleged that punches were actually thrown.

The union was now divided and the Tory Government was on the verge of victory.

When it came to the vote, it was almost too close to call, but the final count was 98 votes to 91 and the strike was finally called off. Two days later at Durham pits, in common with their colleagues in England, Wales and Scotland, miners marched behind union banners to the accompaniment of the colliery band.

This was not a proud moment for the people of Blackhall, Horden or Easington. They knew the strike had failed. Women wept openly in the streets as their men, broken by the Government, went back to work. This marked the beginning of the end for many collieries.

Maggie Thatcher had won, as she had been confident she would do, having put a strategy in place that would literally starve the miners into submission. She had beaten Argentina in 1982 and so the NUM was small fry in comparison.

However, as the New Year arrived in 1985, and with his mates either out of work or on strike, Brian Honour received some good news. He had been a lot happier since he had started playing for Peterlee Newtown in August 1984 and had regularly received Man of the Match awards. Whatever the hardships, he was playing football.

Hartlepool Come Calling

In 1912 the *Titanic* left Southampton Docks for her maiden voyage to New York. Events conspired against the ill-fated ship and the rest, as they say, is history. Various theories have been put forward in the 96 years since the ship's tragic demise, but the one consistent factor regarding the vessel's collision with the iceberg is the part played by fog.

As the thick fog descended on the Atlantic Ocean that fateful night, the ship's lookouts, hindered by the white blanket all around them, failed to spot the frozen mass ahead of them until it was too late. But for the fog, it's likely that the *Titanic* may have avoided the iceberg and the legend would never have been created - and so it is with Brian Honour.

Billy Horner, the then manager of Hartlepool United, had gone to watch a game at Tow Law. Peterlee Newtown were playing and Horner had been tipped off about a player called Keith Fairless.

After less than 30 minutes of play, a thick mass of white fog came to rest on the muddy Tow Law pitch, and the usually biting north-east wind failed to clear what is known colloquially as 'a real pea-souper'.

Keith Fairless was playing in the centre of the pitch and, like the iceberg in the Atlantic Ocean back in 1912, he simply could not be seen. Fairless's chance to shine came and went, and he too sank without trace, condemned to the depths of non-League football forever.

However, one man's tragedy is another man's triumph, and as it happened it was a blessing in disguise for Brian.

Billy Horner did manage to spot something that caught his eye through the foggy gloom on that cold night in the northeast. A few feet from the touchline he noticed a diminutive winger jinking through the mist up and down the wing. In a region that later inspired the film *Billy Elliott*, the Hartlepool boss watched awestruck as the young man hopped, skipped and jumped over tackles. It was footballing ballet, and it would change Brian Honour's life forever.

Obviously the Pools boss was impressed by what he saw. Harry Wilson, who was also at Pools and knew Brian's brother John who had also been at Victoria Ground, as it was in those days, asked Brian if he would be interested in going for a trial.

Well, Brian Honour was on the dole and playing non-League football, so there really was only one answer!

"Would I like a trial at Hartlepool United?" remarked Brian. "You bet I would!"

Had Brian been handed another lifeline by a Football League club situated only a few miles from his Horden home?

Assistant manager at Peterlee Newtown, Bobby Park, said they were very sad to lose Brian but were grateful for the contribution he had made to the side. Brian had actually planned to play for Peterlee Newtown, but Hartlepool United boss Billy Horner had seen enough to know that here they had a little gem.

Brian played in a friendly at Brandon United for Hartlepool and was still on the dole when he turned up for training at Pools on the Thursday. When he walked into the changing room, to his surprise he found his name on the team sheet for that Saturday's game against Peterborough.

Brian didn't actually get paid a single penny for first two games he played for Hartlepool, as he was still on benefits. He travelled to Hartlepool on the X5 from Horden using his Jobseekers bus pass. However, he was able to sign off the dole when Pools gave him a contract until the end of the season.

That first game at home against Peterborough was not the baptism he had hoped for, with the Posh running out winners 3-0. But in the remaining home games Pools beat Wrexham 2-1, Torquay United 3-1, Stockport County 5-1, Colchester United 2-1 and Aldershot 1-0.

Statistics show that in that 1984-85 season Brian played for

Hartlepool United on the right wing 17 times. In April, just two months after signing for Hartlepool United, he was named Player of the Month after averaging marks of 7.80 over five games ahead of several established players including Bob Newton of Chesterfield, who would later play with Brian at Pools.

If Hartlepool wanted to improve their League position they would have to have more wins on the road. But Brian was back in League football and playing only a stone's throw from Horden.

Brian Honour's roller-coaster affair with football continued.

Ever Ready Brian

If Brian only managed 17 appearances in his first season with Pools, in which the team finished 6th from bottom, his first full season, 1985-86, would be the complete reverse, as he would play every one of the 46 League games.

Brian is pictured in the team photocall sitting next to Tommy Johnson, the Pools physiotherapist, in a team that included Keith Nobbs, David Linighan, Roy Hogan, Paul Dobson, Alan Shoulder and Bob Newton.

However, Brian was soon on his way back to Darlington as part of the Hartlepool United team that would play the Quakers in the Durham Senior Professional Cup.

In the first real attack, Kevin Dixon fired in a cross that the defence failed to clear and Brian Honour was there to stroke the ball home. Dixon made it 2-0 and on 14 minutes the team should have gone three up but Shoulder just failed to connect with a Bob Newton cross. Shoulder did score a third before Darlington were handed a dubious lifeline. A penalty of doubtful origin was hit high over the bar by David McLean. Hartlepool scored a fourth goal to put Darlington out of their misery in the 27th minute when Dixon scored again, making it 4-0 going into the break. The second half was a non-event and even the 74th-minute goal from Gary McDonald was nothing more than a consolation.

The League programme kicked off at Cambridge United and although Shoulder and Bob Newton scored for Pools the home side slotted home four. Pools would start the season in 18th place.

On 21st August Pools travelled to Derby County in the League Cup, going down 3-0 before the biggest crowd, 8,419, at the Baseball Ground. The second leg was at the Vic on 4th September and goals from Linighan and Hogan saw Pools win but go out on aggregate 3-2. The result might not be as bad as it first appears, as Derby County were promoted at the end of the season. Hartlepool links with Derby go back to the days of Jack Howe, the old Third Division North battles and, of course, Brian Clough, John McGovern and Tony Parry.

Back at the Vic on 24th August Shoulder and Newton were on target again in a 4-1 win over Crewe Alexandra, but only 2,160 fans saw the rout. Attendances in that season were down nationwide and when Pools played at Chester two days later only 1,473 saw Pools draw. They were beginning to pick up points on the road - something that had deserted them in the previous season. But a defeat to Leyton Orient 2-1 on 31st August and a 2-0 defeat at Burnley saw Pools slump to 20th.

This was not the start that either the fans or Brian wanted.

However, things were about to change, and four wins on the bounce, three at home, to Rochdale, Northampton Town and Swindon and a 3-1 away win to Torquay United saw Hartlepool move up to 6th from top. The attendances continued to cause all clubs in the League anxiety, with only 946 people turning up at Torquay. Pools struck twice within 13 minutes. A flag kick from Honour was met by the head of John Borthwick after eight minutes, and then five minutes later Brian out-jumped the Torquay defence to head home off the inside of the post.

Yes, Brian could head the ball too. He would often out-jump the big fellas in defence.

Torquay pulled one back before the interval through Dawkins to go into the break only 2-1 down. In the 49th minute Brian Honour latched on to a mistake from Compton to beat the keeper from a narrow angle.

Journalist Reg Young gave Honour top marks of 8/10, and in the game against Swindon Town, although Dobson scored the only goal of the game, Brian was once again Man of the Match, attracting a score of 9/10 from sports writer David Wyman.

In the four wins in a row, Brian would score three times against Northampton Town and two at Torquay United.

In September Brian was voted Player of the Month by

Hennessy, the cognac sponsors.

The team came down to earth with a bump, however, when they travelled to Port Vale and crashed 4-0. As it happened, the result was perhaps to be expected as Vale were also promoted come May.

The five games in October would include four wins, with Pools scoring eight goals and conceding five. Brian scored in the 3-1 away at Stockport, supported by Gollogly and Shoulder. The team momentarily touched the heady heights of 3rd place before settling back down to 5th at the end of the month.

Attendances improved in November and on 2nd November 4,195 came to the Vic to see the match with Mansfield Town, one of the other sides to be promoted. Hogan scored Pools' goal in the 1-1 draw. By the end of November 1985 Pools had dropped back into 3rd place after a 1-0 win over Tranmere Rovers with a goal from Walker.

On 7th December in the second round of the FA Cup Pools crashed 1-0 at home to Frickley, with over 4,000 in the Vic - a bitter disappointment to all. Predictably, at the next home League game on 14th December only 2,161 turned up to witness the 4-1 thrashing of Colchester United, the previous result obviously affecting the crowd.

Football writer Mark Dobson posed the question, "Could Pool make it to Division Three?" But he did feel Pool would have to strengthen their squad to make a serious challenge.

For the match on New Year's Day at home to Halifax more than 3,000 turned up to blow away the Hogmanay cobwebs. Two goals from Shoulder set Pools on their way to an easy victory to go back into a promotion place. The team remained unbeaten in the League throughout January and the crowds levelled off at over 3,000. Brian Honour and Alan Shoulder both scored three goals as Pools held on to 4th spot.

On 11th January Pools were away at Leyton Orient whilst the Victoria Ground was covered in snow, with ice beneath the white blanket. Honour again was on hand to slot home the equaliser 11 minutes from time, but Eddie Blackburn took the

Man of the Match award on this occasion with 8/10 from reporter Fred Bell. Eddie had made save after save to keep the London side out.

A week later Cambridge United were the visitors to the Vic. Over 3,300 attended the game and Brian scored twice. His first goal in the 37th minute appeared to be deflected, but this was long before the days of the dubious goal panel and so it was credited to him. Brian scored again on 65 minutes with a superb lob that left the Cambridge keeper Hansbury stranded. Blackburn turned from hero to villain when he fouled Sprigg and Massey converted the penalty. Newton put the ball in the net, thinking he had restored Pools' advantage, but the goal was ruled as offside. However, Hartlepool held on to win 2-1.

On 28th January Brian scored twice along with teammate Lester as Pools beat York in the Associate Members Cup. This match attracted little interest except from the truest blue fans, with only 1,080 turning up on that winter's night.

Two home wins against Burnley and Preston pushed Pools up to 3rd place and promotion looked a distinct possibility.

However, March turned out to be a miserable month with defeats at Peterborough United, Northampton, Swindon and Halifax Town. Two subsequent draws at home to Stockport and Exeter saw the team slump to 6th place.

April Fool's Day brought even more distress for the home fans as Scunthorpe United went away 1-0 winners. The blow was softened, however, when on 11th April Pools beat Southend 3-2, with Brian again being awarded Man of the Match by journalist David Wyman.

The trip to Aldershot provided some additional comfort, as Walker scored for Pools before just 1,277 fans and another point was gained at Hereford United when Brian Honour and Hogan scored for Pools in a 2-2 draw.

Brian was on the score sheet again in the 3-2 win over Southend, but the attendance had dropped to under 1,950, the fans having decided that promotion was again out of reach.

Hartlepool United 3 Southend United 2
12th April 1986
Football League Division Four

This match is unlikely to be remembered for anything other than Brian's sizzling volley. A goal down at the break, Pools rallied in the second half following some harsh words from the then manager Billy Horner. Brian set up the first goal for Alan Little before scoring his eleventh goal of the season when he hit a magnificent 30-yard volley that curled into the top right-hand corner. Winger Nigel Walker added goal number three.

Alan Little had won the FA Youth Cup with Aston Villa, beating Liverpool in the final. He played just three times for Villa in the League and then plied his trade at Southend United, Barnsley, Doncaster Rovers, Torquay United and Halifax Town before turning out for Pools on a dozen occasions. He went on to manage York City, Southend United and Halifax Town.

On 15th April the attendance dropped again to 1,348, but Pools won again, beating Torquay United 1-0. Three days later, however, Pools crashed 4-2 at Tranmere Rovers, 4-0 at Mansfield and 3-1 at Colchester United.

Mansfield were promoted along with Swindon, Chester and Port Vale, with Pools once again finishing as an also-ran just nine points off the automatic promotion place.

However, when Hennessy Cognac invited footballers from the north-east to attend their Footballer of the Year Presentation Dinner at the Civic Centre, Newcastle, on 30th April 1986, in conjunction with the *Evening Gazette*, a few familiar names were amongst the usual suspects: Peter Beardsley of Newcastle United; Mark Proctor and Barry Venison of Sunderland; David McCreery of Newcastle; Tony Mowbray and Gary Pallister from Middlesbrough; Gary McDonald of Darlington; and Brian Honour from Hartlepool.

Yes, after one season with Hartlepool United Brian Honour was up there with the best.

The principal guest that evening was the legendary Bob Stokoe, Sunderland's 1973 Cup winning manager, then at

Carlisle United. Bob was about to retire after 25 years as a football manager.

Later, on 25th May 1986 at the Palm Court Suite in the Staincliffe Hotel, Seaton Carew, Hartlepool United held a Sportsman's Dinner with guest speakers Kevin Keegan, Alan Wright and Bob 'The Cat' Bevan, all hosted by Master of Ceremonies Paul 'Goffy' Gough. Tickets were priced at £12.50, which would hardly buy you the bottle of wine these days. Brian Honour picked up the Hartlepool Supporters Association Player of the Year award ahead of Alan Shoulder, Tony Smith and Nigel Walker.

Brian's third invitation to the 1986 Footballer of the Year Awards was at the Billingham Arms Hotel, Billingham, with guest speakers Wilf McGuinness, the former Manchester United manager, and Gordon Banks and Harold Shepherdson, who were described as 'The Mexico Experts'. Brian collected yet another trophy, as did Tony Mowbray from Middlesbrough.

Another Roller-coaster Ride

The team photograph for the new season, 1986-87, makes interesting viewing, as in addition to the players it also features Malcolm Kirby the secretary, George Lormor, Mick Gough from the famous sporting Gough family who have represented the town at cricket and football, Chairman John Smart, Mick Brown, Malcolm Lancaster, who would later run Brian's testimonial year committee, Alan Bamford, all the directors of the club and Alan Stevenson the commercial director.

The pre-senior games included a 1-1 draw with Sunderland and a 7-0 win in the Durham Senior Cup final against Darlington.

The highlight for Brian during the closed season was his wedding to his childhood sweetheart Janet. It was his 'match of the day'.

Brian and Janet were married at Our Lady Star of the Sea Church in Horden. Brian's best man was a miner, Peter Hallett, a very good friend who sadly is no longer with us. Janet was attended by Paula and Helen Honour, Brian's nieces; Haley Graham, Janet's niece; Karen Roberts, Janet's cousin; and two page boys, Jonathon Honour and Gary Roberts.

The reception was held at the Horden Miners' Welfare and the entertainment was provided by Paul 'Goffy' Gough. Goffy was starting out on a career that would see him hold anchor spots on Century FM and other radio stations in the north as well as advertising a well-known factory floor covering on the telly. Paul and Brian would meet many times in the years ahead, usually when 'Goffy' was presenting him with a supporters' Player of the Year award.

So the young girl coming home from school whom Brian used as target practice was now his wife, and Brian was looking forward to life with his new bride in their first home together. Brian says he remembers the day as though it were yesterday.

The following day, 29th June 1986, Argentina played West Germany in the World Cup final. Jose Brown put Argentina ahead midway through the first half and Jorge Valdano scored a second for the Argies in the 55th minute. The Germans pulled one back through Karl-Heinz Rummenigge in the 74th minute and ten minutes from time Rudi Voller equalised. Seven minutes were left on the clock when a brilliant pass from Maradona gave Jose Burruchuga the opportunity to score the winner for Argentina. Eight years after they won the trophy on home soil, Argentina regained the World Cup and 30 million people celebrated in the streets. Maradona was the Golden Ball winner as the best player in the tournament, while Gary Lineker won the Golden Boot award as leading scorer in the World Cup with six goals.

Brian Honour, on the first day of his honeymoon, watched the World Cup Final on television. A romantic and a true professional!

The Honour house at 20 Meadow Avenue, Blackhall, would be the family home for the next 16 years before they made the move to the 'posh end' of Blackhall within kicking distance of Brian's old school, now a residential establishment for older people. Meadow Avenue was a two-up two-down terrace and the couple would make it a love nest in which to raise the next generation of 'little Honours'.

Unfortunately, during the first few months of marriage Brian did not score many times either on the pitch or off it. In the summer of 1986 he contracted chickenpox, which for an adult in those days could be quite serious. He was really ill. He then broke his wrist, dislocated a bone in his back, broke his nose and sustained a cut that became infected and required hospital-isation.

This marriage lark is not all it's cracked up to be, thought young Brian.

He had to put up with all the usual jokes about married life from his teammates as he struggled with his health. Marriage for Brian and Janet Honour, like his football career, has had its ups and downs. But more than 20 years later Janet and Brian are still together in their little love nest in Blackhall Colliery.

The 1986-87 season was something of an anticlimax on the football front, with Pools failing to score in 18 games in all competitions. In defence, apart from the 5-0 home defeat to Crewe Alexandra and the defeat to Wolves at Molyneaux, Hereford and Cardiff, Hartlepool would lose eight games by just the odd goal. Those 24 points would have given Pools 5th place instead of the abysmal 18th place they achieved. But football isn't about ifs and buts, it's about goals!

Brian scored in consecutive games in the 2-1 win over Torquay United and the 2-0 win over Rochdale, each time supported by a goal from K. Dixon. However, he played only 25 times, plus seven as sub, due to injury and ill health.

In January 1987 Brian submitted a transfer request, which the manager, John Bird, reluctantly accepted. Brian was disappointed with his form and had been unable to secure a regular place. The final straw, Brian recalls, was when Bird signed Terry Cochrane. The 34-year-old was a class player and would occupy Brian's position on the wing.

The writing, he felt, was on the wall.

Mark Wallace, a supporter from Hartlepool, in a letter to the local *Mail* wrote:

"I am number one supporter of Hartlepool Football Club. I was shocked to read that Brian Honour wants to leave the club. I am angry that John Bird got Terry Cochrane to play for Pool. Bird tried to get a good player to push Brian Honour out of the team, that is wrong.

"In the second half of the Burnley game when Terry Cochrane was left out and the right man, Brian Honour, came on, Pool played great. I was glad he was on the pitch. Terry played terrible. He missed easy chances, but when Brian came on Pool got it right. I know Burnley fans were surprised that Pool came back to draw, thanks to the great Brian Honour.

"Best wishes to Brian if he does move but I hope he will stay."

Well, Mark Wallace need not have worried. Despite having broken his wrist in the home win over Exeter City and been given a run out in the reserves in a 3-0 win over Consett in May, Brian Honour relented and signed a new one-year contract for Hartlepool after a clearing the air with manager John Bird.

As it happened, Mr Cochrane would play just two more games for Hartlepool. Yes, he had been a great player in his time, he had cost Middlesbrough almost £250,000 and he was an international with Northern Ireland, but George Best he was not. Coming to Hartlepool in 1987 at the age of 34 years, he was well past his sell-by date. For anyone to think he could replace Brian Honour was foolish.

Despite all his injuries and illness, none of those hurt as much as when he was fully fit and John Bird dropped him. After all, Brian just wanted to play football.

However, in his private life Janet supported her new husband and the couple would face the next season together and look forward to starting a family.

Who's the Daddy?

The 1987-88 season started with a BANG!

Hartlepool met Darlington again in the Durham Senior Cup and again put the Quakers to the sword. Less than 1,900 turned out for the opening game of the season against Newport and witnessed a goalless draw.

Rob McKinnon scored for Pools at Wrexham but Pools lost 2-1.

Then back to the Vic and a bigger crowd was expected for the derby with Darlington. However, it did not transpire. Only 1,808 fans saw Pools thrashed 5-2 by the Quakers. Defeat to the 'old enemy' is difficult to swallow at any time, but by such a large margin and before home fans it hurt Brian - very badly.

Before Pools went to Carlisle on 12th September they had only two points to show from a possible 15 and there was grumbling on the terraces.

Pools turned in a superb performance with a goal from Andy Toman and a brace from Paul Baker. Baker was to score in seven consecutive games as Hartlepool United went on a seven-match unbeaten run, picking up 17 points and moving up to 6th in the League.

On 19th September they beat Colchester United 3-1. The press reported that Dennis Smith, the Sunderland boss, was watching Brian with a view to taking him to Roker Park. Ultimately, not doing so would haunt Smith.

Andy Toman then took over the scoring mantle and he too scored goals with remarkable regularity. By the time the old year was coming to an end, Baker had netted 15 goals and Toman 9. Pools ended the year in 12th place.

In November Pools had pulled a banana skin out of the FA Cup hat - an away try at Chorley. Baker and Gibb scored for Pools without reply to set up a second round encounter with

York City at Bootham Crescent. Many Pools fans made the trip that cold December day. Paul Baker scored for Pools in the 1-1 draw, bringing the Minstermen back to the Vic.

On 9th December two goals from Andy Toman and a third from Paul Baker sent Pools into the third round and York City back down the A19 with their tail between their legs.

Pools pulled Luton Town in the third round. Luton won the day 2-1, with Toman scoring a consolation goal for Pools. More than 6,000 packed the Vic on 9th January 1988 for another great pay day for the club, although not the result everyone wanted.

Brian Honour had a great game. Mark Dawson's report concludes:

"With little Brian Honour showing skill, as well as his combative qualities Pool kept up the pressure. Brave battling by Brian got Paul Baker through and the 20 goal striker rolled the ball over the line only to see the linesman raise his flag. Mark Stein and Danny Wilson (Hartlepool's manager in later years) also went near before The Hatters had the ball in the net twice in a minute. Both goals were disallowed, Mark Stein penalised for pushing, but the writing was on the wall. Half-time 0-0.

"Four minutes after the restart Luton netted again and this time it counted.

"The goal rattled Pool and Mark Stein should have scored twice in the next few minutes.

"Hartlepool sent on John Tinkler for Gibb but Luton's second goal came on 73 minutes. Darren McDonough curled a shot out of the reach of Pools keeper Carr, who the press rather unkindly gave a miserable 5/10.

"Pools did pull one back when Rob McKinnon made a good run and led to a shot from Tinkler which was only half blocked. Andy Toman followed up to net from close range."

Brian Honour was booked for an off-the-ball incident and could have collected a second as he clashed with fullback Breacker. But the only thing Brian collected that night was another Man of the Match award and a mark of 9/10 from reporter Mark Dawson.

In subsequent rounds Luton, playing in the top flight, would face Southampton, QPR and Portsmouth before losing in the semi-final to the MK Dons or, as they were then known, Wimbledon. As history now reveals, Wimbledon's crazy gang would beat Liverpool 1-0 in the final on 14th May.

On New Year's Day Pools went to Feethams and came away with a 1-1 draw, with Paul Baker again scoring. However, their matches in the League during January produced only one goal, scored by John Borthwick, which hardly displayed promotion form.

There was some good news for Hartlepool fans, however, as John Bird announced that Brian had signed an extension to his contract, which would keep him at the Victoria Ground until 1990.

But first there was a trip to Sunderland, who had made enquiries about signing the little lad from Horden.

Stigma for Sunderland

It was a minor distraction for Brian and his teammates when on 9th February 1988 Pools travelled north up the A19 to take on near neighbours Sunderland in an Associated Members Cup game. The crowd at Roker Park was 8,976, which was less than Hartlepool United would take to Sunderland in an FA Cup match many years later.

The conditions at Sunderland were as per normal: windswept, miserable and raining. The prize for the winners was a Northern Area semi-final against Preston North End. Manager Dennis Smith approached the game with his usual arrogance, expecting the Black Cats to sweep aside their 'poorer' neighbours. After all, Sunderland would be promoted as Champions come the end of the season and, as Smith said, "It's only Hartlepool."

However, one man made the arrogant Smith eat his words.

Gale-force winds played havoc in this match, but Pool had still looked dangerous all night, although they could not finish off their battling efforts.

After 79 minutes, Pool received only their second corner, which Brian stepped up to take.

Brian says, "I knew I had to beat the first defender."

He sent his kick curling towards Baker and John Borthwick, but the blustery wind took hold of the ball. It floated over the crowd of players in the six-yard box and back-pedalling goalkeeper Iain Hesford could not prevent the ball from dropping inside the far post.

Hartlepool United 1, Sunderland 0 - and very bitter.

This was Dennis Smith's response when interviewed by the local TV after the game: "If you show that goal - well, you will never get another interview with me!" And to this day, although the TV cameras were there to witness Brian Honour scoring against Sunderland, it has yet to be shown on the box.

Frank Johnson, reporting on the game, quoted Dennis Smith as saying, "It is a disgrace to the club and the lads know it." However, in the first 43 minutes Sunderland didn't create a single chance. 'Only sing when you're winning' springs to mind! Smith described the defeat as a 'stigma'. More like sour grapes!

Colin Diball, in his sports column, used the popular headline "Gone with the Wind" to report that this was only Sunderland's second defeat in 15 League and Cup games and it was all down to the little fella's in-swinging corner. Red faces at Roker Park matched the club shirts.

Brian regards this as his goal of the decade, although he coyly admits, "It was just a fluke really." Never one to hide his love for the Magpies, Brian revelled in his goal, which beat deadly rivals Sunderland and put Hartlepool into the Northern semi-finals. This was his first goal of the year and in Brian's eyes defiantly worth waiting for. Later in the season Sunderland were promoted as champions, so Brian's goal had beaten the best their division had to offer.

In the semi-final Preston North End, playing in the same division as Sunderland, came to the Vic and did a professional job, winning 2-0. Just under 5,000 turned out, which probably indicated that a successful team, or one that was consistently so, would bring back the crowds.

Although these were without doubt memorable and spectacular goals, Brian will be remembered for his 'never say die' attitude and sheer commitment to the club, which rightly earned him the name 'Mr Hartlepool United' from his army of fans.

Bird Says No to Stork

In March, Pools had a mini tour to the south-west of England when the fixture list required them to play Exeter City and Torquay United. In those days the 'little man at the FA' with his pencil and rubber would try to avoid the less fashionable clubs incurring undue expense, so Hartlepool played in Devon over a few days to keep travelling costs to an absolute minimum.

The upside was that it also gave the team 'a little holiday'. However, it was one vacation that Brian could have done without.

Brian had asked manager John Bird if he could stay at home, as his wife Janet was about to give birth to their first child. However, having considered Brian's application he refused his request and Brian was required to make the long journey.

Brian was thus forced to stay away from home for four days when his young wife needed her man. And this wouldn't be the first or last sacrifice the Honours would make in the name of football.

Brian and Janet's family rallied round and they held the young woman's hand as their first child, Sarah, came into the world. Brian was spending the night in Torquay when Sarah was born. However, he rang Janet on the hour, every hour, whilst he was away from home serving Hartlepool United.

It's a wonder he didn't call the little girl 'Victoria', as he spent so much time at the ground and playing for Pools.

Janet describes in her own words later, in the chapter on Brian's testimonial, her thoughts and reflections on his career.

Baker, Toman and Borthwick continued to find the net in the League and a mid-table finish in 16th place again was somewhat disappointing.

Only 823 fans bothered to turn up for the final game of the season. Could the club ever hope to survive on such crowds?

There's Only One United

Brian Honour missed the Durham Senior Cup final with Darlington, having picked up a knee injury at Alloa.

On 24th August 1988, in a pre-season friendly, Hartlepool United beat Manchester United, their FA Cup 1957-58 opponents almost thirty years earlier, 6-0. Fortunately Brian had recovered in time to play in this match.

Had United fielded a weakened team? Well, if Viv Anderson, Paul McGrath, Lee Sharpe and Chris Turner, later to manage Hartlepool United, constituted a weakened team - well, yes it was!

The team was out to prove that the result against quality opposition was not a fluke, and by the end of September Hartlepool United sat proudly in 2nd place in the League thanks to five wins out of seven.

Andy Toman kicked off the season with a 1-0 win at Lincoln City, then scored again in the 2-1 win over Darlington at the Vic. The long trip to Torquay was a fruitless exercise, losing 2-0, but wins over Orient and Cambridge at the Vic came either side of another away day to Bootham Crescent. On 20th September Russell Doig, Dixon and Brian scored the goals in a 3-2 win.

However, in October the wheels came off the promotion bandwagon. Hartlepool, with only two goals from Baker and Barratt, took just one point out of a possible 18. This was not promotion form. The team were in free fall and went from 2nd to 19th in just over five weeks.

On 1st October 1988 John Bird jumped ship and went to York City. His win percentage ratio at Pools was 35%, but at Bootham Crescent it dropped to 29%, which all goes to prove that the other man's grass isn't always greener - just a different shade!

Bob Moncur and 'Pop' Robson took over at the Vic. Moncur had been the only Newcastle United captain in recent years to get his hands on some silverware when they won the Fairs Cup in 1969. Incredibly, Bobby scored a hat-trick over the two legs against the Hungarian side Uspest Doza and Newcastle won on aggregate 6-2. Moncur also captained his native Scotland and played in the 1974 FA Cup final, his last game for the Magpies. Liverpool won 3-0 at the old Wembley Stadium, with a goal from Steve Heighway and, ironically, two from Kevin Keegan.

Bob Moncur had made 358 senior appearances at Newcastle and the fans were hoping that his partnership with Pop Robson signalled a change in fortunes.

November was not much better, however, and although Grayson scored in consecutive games against Peterborough, Grimsby and Exeter only one point in the month was not good enough. The indifferent form continued in the League, but there was some respite for the long-suffering fans in the FA Cup. On 19th November Hartlepool played Wigan Athletic, and goals from Smith and John Borthwick saw Pools win at home 2-0 before a crowd of just under 2,500.

In round two they drew out of the black bag Notts County and on 10th December Joe Allon gave Pools fans an early Christmas present. He scored the only goal before an increased crowd of 3,182 to set up a third round tie with Bristol City. City were in the division above Pools, but a Paul Baker penalty put the home side through 1-0 to set up a fourth round tie with Harry Redknapp's Bournemouth.

Brian Honour had another good game against Bristol and tortured the future England manager Steve McLaren, dispossessing him on several occasions. He left McLaren in his wake.

On New Year's Eve 1988, after a 2-1 win at Colchester United, Pools had managed to pull themselves up to 13th.

In the middle of the FA cup run, however, former manager

John Bird, who at this time was still at York City, came in with an unsettling bid for Rob McKinnon, reported to be £50,000, and an undisclosed amount for Honour. Bird had £100,000 to spend and knew the Hartlepool players like the back of his hand.

Bob Moncur admitted that John Bird had spoken to him about the players but made no offer. In his opinion, "None of Hartlepool's players are available right now." Bird, who had left in the club in October, concluded by saying, "I think they have a real chance against Bournemouth."

Another 900 was added to the previous round gate versus Bristol, once again giving a clear illustration that success on the pitch would bring back the crowds.

Harry Redknapp's men were playing in the old Second Division and other notable League members that season included Chelsea, Manchester City, Blackburn Rovers, Leeds United, Sunderland, Leicester City and Birmingham - all clubs that would in years to come occupy a Premiership spot.

Harry was a wheeler-dealer in those days too and had assembled a good side, all legal and above board of course. This was a time long before the word 'bung' was every mentioned.

So how many would be in the Vic come 28th January? The answer was 6,240, and in the 1-1 draw our hero, Brian Honour, scored for Pools, latching on to a cross from Joe Allon. The Bournemouth keeper Payton made three world-class saves to keep Pools at bay.

In the end, however, it was the cool head of Luther Blissett that took the tie back to the south coast. The ex-England man was sent sprawling in the area following a Tony Barratt tackle. Blissett, the target of a hail of bananas from some of the mindless yobs in the crowd, kept his cool and slotted home the penalty himself.

It was the first goal Hartlepool had conceded in the FA Cup.

After the game, press reports appeared valuing Brian at £150,000, with Reading, Ipswich, Manchester United and Aston Villa all having made enquiries about Pools players, including McKinnon, Tinkler and Brian.

Brian Honour was included in the FA Cup team of the week, along with Mark Hughes from Manchester United, McNab from Manchester City and Robert Fleck from Norwich City, so he was in very good company indeed.

The club's financial position was still perilous, however, and it seemed only a matter of time before somebody would have to leave.

Bob Moncur said, "We need to survive, but more importantly there are promising youngsters here who are capable of stepping in and doing a good job."

Moncur was only too aware of the interest from top clubs. He tied the in-form Honour to Pools until mid-1991 and did similar deals with Rob McKinnon and John Tinkler.

In Brian's case, as history would prove, Moncur had done him a great favour, as when Cyril Knowles arrived at the club from Darlington via Torquay he once again tried to persuade Brian to give up his dream of professional football.

Moncur was then to add Paul Dalton from Manchester United on loan, clearly indicating his ambition.

Preparations were made for the long trip south three days later and many coaches left Hartlepool for the seven-and-a-half hour journey. I was on one of the supporters' coaches with another Pools stalwart, John Mason, with whom I had attended school at Dyke House.

Pools had left the day before and stayed overnight on the south coast to prepare for arguably the most important game in the club's history. The police would not allow Hartlepool fans into Bournemouth much before the kick-off. They disembarked from the buses, watched the match and returned straight to the buses, which arrived back in Hartlepool well after 2 a.m.

Yes, the match was a disappointment and, although Toman and Joe Allon scored, Bournemouth ran out winners 5-2 and would face Manchester United in the next round. The crowd was 10,142 and in the stand, running his seasoned international eye over the game, was Sir Bobby Charlton.

It was apparent to anyone who watched Hartlepool United in that season that with players such as Andy Toman, Joe Allon, Brian Honour, Paul Baker, Paul Dalton, Rob McKinnon and others, if the right blend and mix were achieved and tuned Hartlepool could be knocking on the promotion door.

As soon as Pools were out of the cup Ian Brantfoot, the Reading manager, asked Moncur to accept Mick Tait, an experienced midfielder, plus cash to a total of £125,000 to take either Brian Honour or Rob McKinnon.

At that time Janet Honour was expecting their second child and, taking into consideration the high cost of living in Berkshire, Brian decided it would be better to stay at Pools. He concluded by saying, "I am benefiting from 'Pop' Robson's coaching and in a few years' time we could be above Reading in the League."

Hindsight is a wonderful mistress, of course, and on this occasion Brian would eventually be proved wrong, as Reading would go on to ply their trade in the Premiership, guided by Steve Coppell.

The fans had a long wait and sadly 1988-89 was again not to be the year, as the team finished in 19th place with 20+ defeats. The only consolation for Hartlepool fans was that the 'old enemy' Darlington had an even worse record, winning only three home games at Feethams and losing their League status.

Brian, as ever, felt sorry for the club that had given him a 'free transfer'. The Darlington fixtures were always the first ones he looked for and he felt desperately sorry for everyone at Darlo.

When it was apparent that Hartlepool would not be going up, Brian Honour was advised to have an operation on his knee to remove a piece of torn cartilage, using new techniques of arthroscopy surgery. It was expected that Brian would be fully fit for the start of the new campaign.

Injury Threatens Brian's Career

Brian had been injured in a game at Orient on 21st March 1989 and the following month he was back in hospital again. This time, however, it was to the Maternity Unit at Cameron's Hospital.

Again Brian's photographic memory recalls that the date was 15th April 1989, the day Nottingham Forest played Liverpool at Hillsborough, a game that resulted in the deaths of 96 Liverpool fans. The Taylor Inquiry into the disaster highlighted several issues and as a result many football stadiums became all-seater and barriers were removed from the front of stands.

So what should have been a totally happy day for Brian was tinged with sadness, as his thoughts, like those of the rest of the country, were with the people of Liverpool who had lost loved ones.

"You don't expect when your fella goes out to a football match, the next thing you hear is a knock at the door and a policeman telling you he is dead," reflected Brian.

But his new baby daughter, Laura, arrived safe and well and, as with her older sister, her godfather was to be Brian's teammate and Scottish International, Rob McKinnon.

Following his operation in May, Brian found himself under the knife again on 24th June at the Nuffield Centre in Norton. He cannot speak too highly of all the medical staff, doctors and nurses who attended him on the numerous occasions he required their help.

Doctor Montgomery, who did Brian's cartilage operation, advised him to quit. But, as any Hartlepool supporter at the time knows, Brian Honour may be many things, but he's certainly not a quitter. "If you keep going you will suffer," said the good doctor, but Brian was never going to pack it in.

With 14 operations on his right knee and 3 on his left foot, this guy had more injuries than Evel Knievel - well, not quite.

Whilst doing some rehabilitation exercises, Brian felt something click and he was in trouble again. He knew that if the subsequent operations were unsuccessful he could end up with arthritis in later life. He went to Hartlepool General and his leg was put in plaster for six weeks. However, when the plaster was removed, it was no better and nothing seemed to work.

Brian was still on the injured list in late 1989 when the cruel hand of fate struck again, and this time he would be out of action for more than nine months.

Cyril Knowles, who had resigned as manager of Torquay United in October after a disappointing start to their season, returned to management with 'basement' club Hartlepool United. When he arrived at the Victoria Ground, Pools were rock bottom in 24th place, a position they would occupy until January 1990.

All good heroes have a nemesis - a person, place or object that haunts their existence and hinders their progression towards greatness. Superman had Kryptonite, The Beatles had Yoko Ono, and George Best found his great rival in various liquid varieties. Brian Honour was no exception; he too had his nemesis.

In late 1989, Hartlepool United's new manager walked onto the training ground to be introduced to his group of players and staff. The Pools squad stood tall, smiled and offered handshakes to their new gaffer - all except for Brian, whose heart sank to the pit of his stomach on seeing that the man was none other than Cyril Knowles.

There was little Brian Honour could do. He would turn up at the club and work with the physio Gary Henderson. He would put in hours every week, but to no avail. The knee would not respond to treatment. Brian felt reasonably secure, however, thinking that the extension to his contract would enable him to be paid and get fully fit.

Unfortunately Mr Knowles had other thoughts. He had brought with him the old school thinking that Brian had witnessed at Feethams. Cyril liked big lads, tall and able to push their weight about, and Brian was never going to be able to fulfil his new manager's expectations.

Brian was summoned to Mr Knowles' office.

"As I walked along the corridor I thought to myself, well it isn't only Father Christmas who is going to get the sack," Brian explained, and then realised there was still plenty of time remaining on his contract, so he should be safe - or so he thought!

"How's the knee?" enquired Cyril.

"Oh, it's not too good," replied Brian.

At this point Cyril asked Brian to remove his tracksuit bottoms and stand in front of a mirror. In the reflection, Brian's knee looked swollen and deformed.

Brian goes on: "Cyril gave me what he thought was sound advice."

"I think I would pack in if I were you," Cyril said, pointing to the redness and swelling.

Cyril Knowles knew all about knee injuries, as it was a similar injury that had ended the former Spurs man's career.

Brian thinks that because he was so popular with the fans Mr Knowles didn't want to terminate his contract. Instead he was inviting the lad to jump rather than be pushed.

This is a fair assumption, as axing Brian would have put Knowles in the same category as the hunters who shot Bambi's mam.

Brian declined the invitation, and on leaving the office went to see Gary Henderson, the club's physiotherapist, to share the conversation he'd just had with the new manager.

All the thoughts of rejection at Aston Villa for being too small and earlier rejection from Cyril Knowles at Darlington came flooding back.

Another Good Doctor

Rightly or wrongly, physio Gary Henderson told Brian, "You are not ready to pack in."

He was right in one respect. Brian was only 24 years old and he had a wife and young family to support. Surely he could manage some exercise!

Gary arranged for Brian to see a specialist at Darlington Memorial, a Dr. Rutherford, and Brian had a few anxious days' wait to see the consultant.

Was this to be the end of the career in professional football that Brian Honour wanted so badly?

Brian knew that the specialist could either make or break both his career and his heart. You get the feeling that Brian would have played football on crutches if that had been allowed. It seems strange, looking back, that a doctor from Darlington, Hartlepool United's most bitter rivals, had one of our favourite sons' career in his hands.

We need not have worried.

Dr. Rutherford took one look at Brian's knee and shook his head, and for a moment Brian's heart skipped a beat and he feared the worst.

"If you come back on Saturday, I think I might have the solution," said the doctor, "and don't worry."

Why do doctors always say that?

Of course Brian did worry. If he could not play football what could he do? The pits had closed, unemployment was high, and with just four GCSEs under his belt prospective employers would hardly be knocking at the door of his home in Meadow Avenue.

He worried for the next few days. They seemed like a lifetime.

Pools were at Scunthorpe as Brian went across to Darlington

to see Dr. Rutherford at the Memorial Hospital. As Brian went under the surgeon's knife, Pools, thanks to Paul Dalton, came away with a 1-0 win, moving the side away from the bottom up to 21st spot.

Cyril would see further wins that season, including a seven match unbeaten run, with Baker, Allon, Olsson and Dalton all hitting the onion bag. The crowds, too, had edged above the 2,500 mark, but Mr Knowles had a lot to do.

Meanwhile, back in the operating theatre, Brian was coming round from the general anaesthetic and his first words were, "How did the lads get on?" Once he'd found out the result he began to feel a lot better, before dozing off again under the prolonged effects of the anaesthetic.

When Dr. Rutherford came back to discharge him, he simply said, "Right, Brian, off you go. Plenty of exercise."

The doctor revealed that behind Brian's knee there had been a great deal of debris picked up over the years as a result of constant kicking from those unfortunate defenders who tried to catch him.

Now the debris had been removed, the doctor's advice was: "Carry on, Brian."

Carry On Brian

During that summer, Brian did manage to have a family holiday. All the family budget would stretch to was a week at Pontins in Blackpool with teammate Paul Baker and his family. Then, instead of sunning himself on the beach and making sandcastles with the kids, for the rest of the summer Brian worked on his fitness. Throughout June, July and well into August, Brian would spend his days running up and down the sand dunes at Seaton Carew and near his home in Crimdon Dene.

He was determined to be fit.

Brian also used the facilities at the Mill House Leisure Centre, and only he and Gary Henderson knew the sacrifices and pain barriers he went through each day in pursuit of physical fitness.

When he returned to Pools after the summer break, the squad went down to Catterick Garrison to one of Cyril's famous 'boot camps'. No matter what they threw at Brian, no matter what test they tried, no matter what race was run, the little fella won everything. His teammates and colleagues were amazed and obviously delighted.

Cyril Knowles, however, was not convinced. He was still hanging on to his philosophy: "I like big lads, who can muscle their way out of this division." Like many managers at the time, he must have thought the only way out of the bottom flight was to kick your way out.

History will tell us that there was a place for skill and in truth size was not an issue; well, it wasn't when you had a heart as big as Brian's.

Brian was in and out of the team, a sub more often than not at first, until the Tottenham Hotspur game in September. By that time Pools were in 23rd position and grumblings from the terraces had reached the boardroom.

When Brian Honour went to White Hart Lane with Pools on 26th September, Hartlepool United were in 22nd place and were facing yet another battle against relegation.

Once again, Brian was left on the bench. In fact, in those early days of the season some of the lads nicknamed Brian 'The Judge' as he spent so much time on the bench.

But things were about to change.

Brian recalls warming up at the start of the match with Spurs when another lad came onto the pitch and saluted the Hartlepool fans.

It was none other than Gazza!

Paul Gascoigne approached the Hartlepool fans to shake hands and wave to the many from the north-east who had made the trip to the capital. They responded by chanting, "Gazza is a Geordie, la la la". The great showman loved it.

Over the next 90 minutes Gascoigne turned in what many neutrals deem to be the greatest individual display ever seen on a football pitch. And when one considers the many memorable performances that certain players have made over the years, this is a bold statement to make.

George Best single-handedly put Northampton Town to the sword in 1970, scoring a double hat-trick. Also in that list is Diego Maradona's virtuoso performance against the Koreans in Mexico in 1986. Hunted by the men from Seoul, who often put as many as six men on him, Maradona turned into a footballing Rudolf Nureyev in front of 60,000 in Mexico City. The three assists he's credited with that day barely tell the story. Even David Beckham's 'Roy of the Rovers' heroics against Greece in 2001 must be considered.

But simply to say that Gascoigne 'ran the show' that night in North London is a colossal understatement. Gazza didn't just call the tune on that pitch, he wrote the music, conducted the orchestra, played percussion, banged the drums, and sang lead vocals. What Paul Gascoigne did with a football that night transcended the boundaries of sport. It was football, it was music, it was poetry … it was art.

However, 90 minutes later when Paul Gascoigne had scored his fourth goal to give Spurs a 5-0 lead to take back to the Victoria Ground in the second leg, the mood was slightly different. Having witnessed first hand what many regarded as the single most amazing thing they'd ever seen on a football pitch, the same Hartlepool United fans who sang "Gazza is a Geordie" as he entered the arena, acknowledged the display as he left it - by pelting him with Mars Bars and chanting "You Fat Bastard!"

Well, as Jimmy Greaves famously said, "It's a funny old game."

Yes, we had lost. But Paul Gascoigne showed that night what potential he had. Sadly, in later years we would watch him waste that talent.

Brian got onto the pitch with only a few seconds to go, but at least he could say he played at Spurs.

The return leg is remembered for other reasons. You couldn't get a ticket for one thing!

More than 9,630 people crammed into the Victoria Ground to see Paul Dalton score in a 2-1 defeat. Brian played, but on his own admission it wasn't one of his best games. However, one man on the Pools side who did play well was Don Hutchinson. Don had a cracking game.

The entrepreneur Chairman Gary Gibson sent videos of Don's performance to every First and Second Division club in the League. Kenny Dalglish would come in for Don and he moved to Anfield for many thousands of pounds - cash that would come in very handy in the years ahead.

So one match probably changed the face of the season.

Hartlepool would eventually lose a young man who had gone through the Pools youth system to the Merseyside giants, and would then go on to play for West Ham, Everton and others and along the way collect 23 international caps for Scotland. That's 23 more than John McGovern, who also started his career at Pools, but then young John has two European Cup winners medals and to date remains the only Scotsman to have lifted the famous trophy twice.

It also perhaps sent a message to Cyril Knowles, and Brian Honour was subsequently included in the Hartlepool line-ups for the rest of the season.

Is it coincidence that the club's rise from 22nd place to 3rd from top and their subsequent promotion were achieved when Brian came back into the team? You may think not.

After the visit by Spurs, the 9,630 attendance numbers dropped dramatically to just 1,900 for Aldershot's visit, so the fans had obviously attended the former match to see the likes of Gazza and Lineker. But Joe Allon popped up with one of his goals and Pools won 1-0. Four days later it was former Manchester United lad Paul Dalton who was on the score sheet when Maidstone lost 1-0.

An away trip to Doncaster gave much-needed evidence that the defence had been tightened up and if the goals kept coming one end and Cyril sorted the defence - which was his speciality - well, who knows?

A reverse at home to York City 1-0 was followed by a draw at Wrexham and wins at home to Peterborough and Hereford United, with Allon and Baker on the score sheet again. Baker scored again at Northampton, as did Fletcher, but Pools lost by the odd goal in five and dropped back to 14th in the League.

On 10th November Pools were at near neighbours Darlington and Joe Allon popped in the only goal before a crowd of 5,000. Baker and Tinkler scored two weeks later at Scarborough in a 2-0 win to take Pools back up to 9th place.

In the intervening week Joe Allon had scored a hat-trick away at Runcorn in the FA Cup, but the run was to come to an end in the next round at Wigan.

Many questions have been asked over the years about Brian Honour's relationship with Joe Allon. There are certain pundits who believe that Brian doesn't like Joe and vice versa. So what is the truth?

Did Joe play the big 'I am' with his big money move to Chelsea, which in truth was not successful? Did Joe point to the fact that he scored all the goals when in fact it was Brian and other members of the team who made them? Or was Joe

Allon, deep down, jealous of Brian Honour and the adulation he attracted from the fans? Oh yes, they chanted "There's only one Joe Allon", but when it came to the crunch the fans overwhelmingly put the little fella ahead of 'Smiling Joe'.

So how does Brian sum up the situation? And what is Joe Allon's response?

Brian first!

"Joe Allon is good company to be with and is always smiling," said Brian.

Joe's response!

"I had the pleasure of his company both on and off the park. His is loved by the players and adored by the fans," replied Joe. "He could easily have played at a higher level."

So there you have it from the two Pools legends. They are good pals to this day. So that's the end of that myth!

Wins at Torquay and at home to Lincoln with all the goals coming from Joe Allon saw Pools move up to 6th place, but still the crowds were disappointing with just over 2,000 in the ground for the Lincoln game.

On the Saturday before Christmas, the Pools players obviously had their minds elsewhere as their wives and girlfriends went Christmas shopping in Manchester, and Hartlepool travelled to Burnley. A 4-0 defeat brought them back down to earth with a bump, and over the Christmas period they had time to contemplate on the following year as the next game was not until New Year's Day at Halifax.

A Happy New Year

The Shay is a notoriously cold ground, with icy winds blowing down off the Yorkshire hills, and Halifax is a miserable place in the summer never mind in January. Nevertheless, our man Joe Allon punched home two goals and Pools won 2-1.

The away trip to Cardiff, as it did many years later, brought nothing but heartache as Pools lost 1-0.

If nothing, this side was resilient and back at the Vic on 19th January Allon scored again, as did Steve Tupling, in a 2-0 win over Chesterfield. The Hartlepool public were still not convinced this was a promotion side with just 2,134 in the ground for the game.

Another trip was made to York City and a 0-0 draw and valuable away point was followed by a 3-1 home win over Stockport County, Paul Baker and Joe Allon again netting the vital goals.

That win added 300 to the attendance at the next home game against Cumbrian rivals Carlisle United. Joe scored one from open play and one from the spot and wingers Paul Dalton and Brian Honour added the others. It was Brian's first goal since 28th August, but his role appeared to be: put the ball on Joe Allon's head, foot or wherever and let him score.

Joe obliged many times that season, but when Joe's goals dried up the team suffered! In a five-match run Pools only picked up two points and Joe only scored once from open play and once from the spot. As a result, the team dropped down to 11th in the table.

On 12th March Pools made the long trip to Aldershot and recorded one of their best away wins of all time. Paul Dalton was unstoppable and scored a hat-trick, with Joe Allon and Tinks scoring one apiece in a 5-1 victory.

However, again Pools seemed to lack the killer punch. On

16th March a Rob McKinnon goal was the only bright spot in a 2-1 home defeat by Blackpool.

Away Form
Baffles Fans

On the road Hartlepool United's form continued to confuse their fans. A trip south to Maidstone on 23rd March 1991 resulted in a 4-1 win, with a goal from Dalton, one from Baker and two from Brian pushing the club up one place. Brian names a goal he scored in this game as one of his best.

Those of you who remember this game may be asking: which goal?

Brian scored two amazing goals in this thrashing of Maidstone at Watling Street. Brian selected goal number two as his third favourite in his Pool career.

The move started with a brilliant show of control by Baker in the centre of the park to lay the ball off to Rob McKinnon. McKinnon's cross caused all sorts of problems to the Maidstone defence and Brian seized his chance, controlling the ball beautifully before drilling his shot past keeper Mark Beeney to rightfully claim his place among the finalists of the North East Goal of the Season competition.

Rob McKinnon, as mentioned earlier, went on to become a Scottish international, playing all his games away from his homeland.

Despite this triumph, Pools were running out of games and needed to climb at least another three places.

Walsall were the visitors on 26th March and Joe obliged with two goals. As a result, the team moved up to 7th but still less than 2,600 saw the match. The Hartlepool public remained unconvinced that this team could go up.

Baker and Allon provide the goals in a 3-1 win at Stockport County on 29th March and a 0-0 draw with Burnley on April Fool's Day attracted just under 5,000. Then on a trip to Walsall on 6th April Joe Allon scored the only goal before three days later Dalton and Baker took over the scoring duties and Scunthorpe were sent back to Lincolnshire, beaten 2-0. Pools were up to 5th place.

Baker and Allon scored in the next game at home to Halifax to move up to 4th place, but a home draw with Doncaster on 16th April with a goal from McPhail was not enough to move up the League.

Games were running out for Brian and his teammates.

When Wrexham visited on 20th April and goals from Baker and Allon sent them back to Wales pointless, the crowd just topped 3,000. This was followed by a goalless draw at Rochdale and a 1-1 draw at Peterborough, who would finish two points behind Pools, which kept the team in 4th place.

Gillingham were the next visitors and a Joe Allon goal saw Pools home and up to 3rd place, the crowd rising to 3,700. It was Joe's 34th goal of the season.

Brian Honour admitted later that his heart was pounding after allowing Gillingham's Manuel his side's best chance after 61 minutes. It was Gillingham's only chance in the game.

Did the Hartlepool public at last realise that here was a winning promotion team?

The Final Push

The strike force of Baker, Dalton and Allon all appeared on the score sheet for the final two games of the season, a 3-1 win at Hereford and that never to be forgotten day on 11th May 1991 when Northampton Town were the visitors.

In that final game, Brian Honour and Paul Olsson worked tirelessly in the midfield for Pools. After a somewhat nervous start, Paul Dalton scored after 17 minutes, but Town's Steve Brown equalised and the sides went in level at half-time. In the second half, Joe Allon put Hartlepool in front on 57 minutes and then three minutes later Paul Baker put the game beyond doubt with a spectacular lob over Peter Gleasure and into the Town goal to seal victory. Hartlepool United had won 3-1 and 6,957 people cheered from the rafters.

Hartlepool celebrated as a town united, except one unhappy punter who felt robbed. David Parker had backed Pools to win when they were 25/1 and his £15 bet should have returned the Pools fan over £350. He ran all the way to the local branch of Ladbrokes to pick up his winnings when Hartlepool United were promoted, but Ladbrokes said there had been a mistake and would investigate and offered the winner each way odds. Two other Hartlepool men, Rollie and Ernie Codling, also felt they had been short-changed.

However, the Hartlepool fans who graced the Vic on promotion day had full value for money.

In the *Mail* on the Monday, the chief reporter at the time, Carol Malia, now the presenter of the BBC's nightly *Look North* programme, wrote under the banner headline "Murray Makers" to describe Pools' momentous day.

A jubilant chairman, Gary Gibson, promised to strengthen the side for the assault on the Third Division title and Don Hutchinson joined his former colleagues at Pools to watch the win over Northampton. People had forgotten that Northampton needed to win to reach the play-offs and hoped that York City would beat Torquay United at Plainmoor.

Brian Honour had played his part once he was given the chance and he had appeared in 39 of the 46 games. One can only speculate what might have happened if he had played those other seven games when Pools only picked up four points from a possible 21.

Joe Allon is credited with scoring the magnificent amount of goals he did in that promotion season, but he would be the first to admit that he had good service from the wingers, Messrs Dalton and Honour.

At the end of the game, Pools came back out onto the pitch to throw various items of clothing to the crowd. Two little boys (not the ones in the song by Rolf Harris, which Hartlepool fans seem to have adopted as their own) were engaged in a tug of war for a sock belonging to Steve Tupling. The more wiry-looking lad is reported to have won.

John Riddle takes up the story:

"I had been to the match with my son David. After the game in the ensuing celebrations we somehow got separated. I made my way home to be followed a few minutes later by David.

"'I've got Steve Tupling's sock,' he gasped and produced a blue sock, I think it was, from under his coat. I swear it was 5 feet in length. He explained the early tug of war and how he'd managed to wrestle the sock from the other lad.

"David was 13 at the time.

"He now tells me the sock was no more than 3 feet and I have embroidered the rest, as I am prone to do.

"But that little lad is now not so little standing over 6 feet tall, still wiry but after an excellent education at English Martyrs School he went off to University. David was appointed to a teaching post in of all places Rushden. But it did come in handy when we played down there in another promotion season, David getting me two priceless tickets for the final game.

"I will always remember the late Paul Mullen, the Hartlepool press officer, walking through the stands and spotting me sitting on the front row with the Rushden fans for company.

"Paul gave one of his knowing smiles and said, 'I am not even going to ask how you got those seats.' I will forever remember Paul's smile.

"David returned to Hartlepool in September 2007 as Assistant Head of Sixth Form at ... yes, English Martyrs Sixth Form college - so he has come full circle.

"We will be at Pools together more often these days, but the players can rest assured - he won't be engaged in a tug of war with any more socks.

"He has assumed new responsibilities these days."

Hartlepool United always has been a family club and anecdotes like this will continue to be told around the pubs and clubs in the town. Father passes the love of Pools down from father to son and thus a solid fan base and a continuation of support is maintained. Of course these days it is passed from mother to daughter as well as more and more lovely ladies become Hartlepool United fanatics.

The Mayor at the time, Councillor John Lynch, added his congratulations to the hundreds of messages that came in from far and wide. It would be one of the Mayor's last acts as he handed over the mayoral chain to fellow Labour Party councillor, Trevor Lloyd, a few days later.

One of the messages received at the time came from the other side of the world. In Perth, Australia, a former Pools and Boro player, Graham Normanton, added his good wishes from his club down under, Kingsway Olympic.

Pools announced the retained list two days later and Cox, Davies, Dunbar and Paul Clarke were all released. The rest of the squad flew off to Majorca for a well-earned break in the sun on a trip prearranged by Pools chairman Gary Gibson. When they returned, Rob McKinnon would sign a new contract.

But could Hartlepool United keep the promotion winning team together? The weeks and months ahead would provide the answers.

During the summer, work started on the new stand along the east side of the ground on Clarence Road - the stand we now call the Cyril Knowles stand.

Cyril was not there to witness the promotion, the culmination of his work, as he was too ill, but the players and fans knew at the bottom of their hearts that, although Alan Murray had guided the team to promotion, it was Cyril Knowles who had laid the foundation.

Nice one Cyril!

A Trip to the Palace

Hartlepool started the 1991-92 season with a trip to Torquay. Paul Baker scored a consolation goal for Pools as Torquay won 3-1. The team started the season in 19th position. Baker was on the spot again when Reading visited Hartlepool on 24th August in the League and a second goal from Olsson saw Pools win 2-0.

Baker scored again in the League Cup at home to Bury, and goals from Gabbiadini and Fletcher in the away leg saw Pools go through 3-2 on aggregate and set up a home tie with Crystal Palace in September.

In the meantime David Rush, who was on loan from Sunderland, scored at Bradford City to earn Pools a point in a 1-1 draw.

Before the match, a Hartlepool official came into the dressing room and announced that Cyril Knowles had passed away. Brian's only regret was that he never had the opportunity to say a last goodbye to the Pools boss who had laid the foundations for promotion.

Cyril Knowles, 1944-1991. May he rest in peace.

On 3rd September Brentford were the visitors at the Victoria Ground. Ricardo Gabbiadini grabbed the only goal to please the crowd of 3,660 and take Pools into 6th place. However, the bubble burst somewhat on 7th September when Leyton Orient were the visitors and, although Rush scored again supported by Paul Dalton, the 'O's' went home with all three points.

A Baker penalty on 14th September saw Pools pick up an away point at Exeter City and the same player scored at Stoke City on 17th September as Pools went down again by an odd goal. Those dropped six points, come the end of the season, would prove vital.

Four days before the big match with Palace, Birmingham City were the visitors to Hartlepool and 'Bakes' scored the only goal before 4,643 fans. It was Paul's sixth goal of the season.

The day before the Rumbelows Cup second round, first leg match against Crystal Palace on 25th September 1991, before a crowd of 6,697, the top-flight London club had waved goodbye to prolific scorer Ian Wright, who had left for Arsenal, but they still had a successful striking partner, Mark Bright, and even had a little-known forward by the name of Stan Collymore on the bench.

Pool did not look overawed by their London opponents, but Palace went ahead in the 11th minute when Bright headed past Martin Hodge. But Pool kept up the pressure and it paid off seven minutes into the second half when Rob McKinnon sent Paul Baker away down the left. The skipper hooked the ball towards the goal mouth, where it was headed down by Paul Dalton. The attendance of two Crystal Palace defenders did not seem to bother Honour, who turned sharply before slamming his shot beyond Nigel Martyn. Brian rates this goal as one of his top five, and was rewarded with a colour television for his performance in the game by the sponsors Rumbelows.

Palace Boss Steve Coppell admitted afterwards, "The little winger had a great game." Steve Coppell had played for England and Manchester United before going on to manage Palace, Manchester City, Brentford, Brighton and Reading, the latter of whom he took to the Premiership. He was also voted the League Managers Association Manager of the Year 2006. So who could argue with his assessment of Brian's performance?

As history now reveals, Mark Bright played 227 games for Palace, scoring 92 goals. Nigel Martyn played more than 700 career games and picked up 23 England caps. Yes, 'our Brian' scored past an England goalkeeper.

Meanwhile, back in the League, a good away point for Pools at Bury with Gabbiadini scoring was followed on 5th October with a home game against Wigan Athletic.

That weekend Alan Price, previously of The Animals and

'House of the Rising Sun' fame, appeared at the Borough Hall. He had left the group behind because of his fear of flying, but it was Hartlepool United who would be flying as we entered October.

David McCreary was relegated to the bench for the game with Wigan as Honour, Dalton and John Tinkler were working so well in midfield. Just four minutes into the game Brian found the net for his first League goal of the season. Pools went into the half-time break 3-1 in front, thanks to two goals from Paul Dalton. After the break, Wigan stormed back and when Daley equalised it looked as if a 3-3 draw would be the result. Enter Rob McKinnon. His strike from distance just two minutes from time gave Hartlepool a 4-3 win.

After the match Rob told fans via the local press that they should not be disappointed if the team did not achieve successive promotions.

Gary Gibson had to deny that he was trying to sell Brian Honour by circulating a video of Brian's recent games. This method had worked before and had netted Pools around £300,000 when Don Hutchinson went to Liverpool. But this tactic would not have worked with little Brian, as he was too quick even for the cameras - he certainly was on 'fast forward' in those days.

The 8th October replay of the game on 25th September, when Pools held mighty Palace to a 1-1 draw, would turn out to be something of an anticlimax. Ricardo Gabbiadini was selected to play for Pools and would face his big brother Marco, whom the London club had recently signed for £1.8m.

Steve Coppell remarked on the club's website that "Hartlepool have nothing to lose and they will raise their game."

Well, Pools didn't raise it enough.

The Eagles were flying high that day as they rattled in six goals, through Bright in the 30th and 71st minutes, big brother Marco, Thom, Gray and Collymore, before Pools did get a consolation. Honour crossed from the right, Fletcher went up, Nigel Martyn pushed it away and John Tinkler was on hand to

Left: Brian, number 8,
Cotsford Junior
School, 1974

Below: Darlington FC
team call, 1983/1984

Above: The Butlin's Boys! 1978

Right: Brian's first contract with
Hartlepool United, 16 May 1985

Hartlepool United
Football Club Limited

Victoria Ground, Hartlepool, Cleveland, TS24 8BZ Tel: (0429) 72564

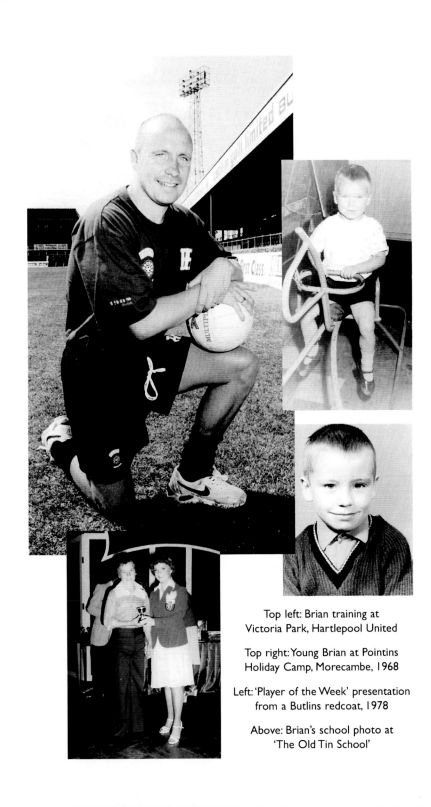

Top left: Brian training at
Victoria Park, Hartlepool United

Top right: Young Brian at Pointins
Holiday Camp, Morecambe, 1968

Left: 'Player of the Week' presentation
from a Butlins redcoat, 1978

Above: Brian's school photo at
'The Old Tin School'

Above: Clive Clark
(West Bromwich Albion) and
Brian 'Player of the Week',
Butlins, 1978

Right: Brian wins The McEwans'
'Player of the Year' Award,
1985/1986

Above: The Player of the Year
guests, Brian, next to legend
Gordon Banks

Right: Brian taking a break
at Hartlepool United's
Victoria Park

Brian's welcome pass
to Villa Park, 1978

Programme, Tottenham Hotspur
v Hartlepool United, 1990

Hughie Hamilton and Tommy Miller

Peter Beardsley and Brian share a joke at Newcastle United

stab the ball home. The 1,000 travelling fans had at last seen something to cheer about, or at least those who had stayed to the end. Crystal Palace, then a top-flight club, won the tie on aggregate 7-2.

The team appeared to be a little deflated after the drubbing at Selhurst Park and lost at Bournemouth 2-0, at Peterborough 3-2 and, worst of all, at local rivals Darlington 4-0 before a crowd of over 5,000. After the match, the Darlington players behaved in an irresponsible manner, banging repeatedly on the Pools dressing room door and singing "4-0, 4-0, 4-0". That hurt everyone, but especially Brian Honour as he had previously been a Quaker.

But not any more!

That was followed by a goalless draw at home to West Brom, but the Cup run had taken its toll and Pools, who had been in 6th place in early September, were now down to 19th.

On 9th November 1991, Hartlepool faced Fulham. Big Mick Smith had returned after suspension and the former Northern Ireland international David McCreary was fit to play despite having stitches under his eye and a broken nose. They did nothing to improve his looks.

The new stand on the east side of the ground was still the subject of delays.

After a turgid first half, the teams trooped off with the score at 0-0. However, the fans did have something to cheer about after the break - Brian Honour scored. Brian had been a thorn in the side of Fulham and blasted home the first goal. It was Pools' first in more than 250 minutes of football.

On loan striker David Johnson had failed a fitness test and so teenager Steve Fletcher retained his place. He added a second goal, restoring Pools to their winning ways, the team having gone six games without a win.

Brian Honour was booked for a foul on Newson, even though the linesman who was standing only a matter of feet away saw nothing. However, the referee, Mr M Peck from Kendal, thought he saw something and the little fella saw yellow.

It was a good result for Pools though - 2-0.

A week later, on 16th November, Hartlepool met Shrewsbury Town in the first round of the FA Cup. Paul Baker was back after serving a three-match ban following his sending off against Hull City. Baker would tuck away a 75th minute penalty to sink the stubborn Shrews.

Shrewsbury had taken a surprise lead after only three minutes when Neil Lynne put them ahead, but John Tinkler was on hand to pull Pools level at half-time. David Johnson, who was on loan at Pools at the time from Sheffield Wednesday, scored but his strike was cancelled out when Mark Smith levelled for Town.

The Shrewsbury goalkeeper Parks then leapt spectacularly to save from Brian before the penalty. Brian was fouled on the edge of the six-yard box as he shaped up to score and Parks, to prevent him scoring, chopped him down. Paul Baker stepped up and scored from the spot.

The following week, as so often happens, Pools played Shrewsbury again, this time in the League away. Dalton, Olsson (2) and Paul Baker scored the goals in an impressive 4-1 win.

And 4-1 was the score at Preston North End on 14th December, with goals from Dalton, Johnson and Baker (2). The most impressive fact about the win at Preston, however, was that Pools played on a plastic pitch - for the first time in six years.

Paul Baker netted after ten minutes, Paul Dalton made it 2-0 after 17 minutes, Baker netted another 27 seconds into the second half and David Johnson scored the fourth goal in the 49th minute. The game was all over in less than an hour. Lee Ashcroft scored a consolation for North End before 5,032 dumbstruck fans and Pools ran out easy winners 4-1. It could have been worse for the Lancashire side though, as Brian had a near-miss when he hit the post, leaving three players in his wake.

Asked after the match what was the difference between grass and Astro Turf, Brian as quick as a flash replied, "I don't know, I have never smoked Astro Turf."

Of course he is alleged to have pinched that little quip from Sir Ian Botham, but in reality I doubt either of them said it. It was more likely just some wag making up a tale.

Happy Days!

On 17th December Pools met Darlington at Feethams in the second round of the FA Cup. There were more than 5,500 at Feethams for this crucial encounter.

Andy Toman, previously of Pools, scored for the home side, but goals from Paul Dalton and Brian would ultimately win the day. A report of Brian's goal indicates that Johnson went round Scott Gregan on the left wing and whipped in a cross. Paul Baker missed it due to its speed and it fell to Brian Honour, who volleyed it home. He then went on an amazing run and dived full length into the rapturous Hartlepool fans. It wasn't the last time his appearance at Feethams would attract the attention!

Hartlepool United had beaten local rivals Darlington - don't you just love saying that? Pools had beaten Darlington and were in the hat for another possible big match.

On 21st December Pools went on a 'smash and grab' raid at Reading, Paul Baker's second-half strike bringing home the bacon in a 1-0 win. On 51 minutes, Brian led the charge up the right, jinked past two defenders with the grace of an 'English' Jimmy Johnstone and crossed the ball to the near post. Paul Dalton flicked it on and there was 'Bakes' to crash home his 12th goal of the season.

The journey back to Hartlepool from Berkshire was a happy one and the win had assured that a bumper crowd would turn out at the Victoria Ground on Boxing Day, when 5,413 saw Paul Baker score again.

On 28th December Torquay United were the visitors and a goal from David Johnson, on loan from Sheffield Wednesday, earned Pools a 1-1 draw. Pools finished the old year in 8th position.

The New Year, however, did not start as the team would have

hoped and they went down 1-0 at Brentford. Some of the players were perhaps thinking about the match at Portman Road on 4th January when Hartlepool would face Ipswich Town in the third round of the FA Cup. Yes, Ipswich had been pulled out of the hat, but Pools were away to the top-flight side.

More than 2,000 Pools fans made the trip to Portman Road for the third round FA Cup match against Ipswich on 4th January, making the total attendance 12,507. John Lyall, the Ipswich boss, had already warned his players to be on 'double guard' against Hartlepool. Ipswich were top of their Division with Blackburn Rovers and so welcomed Pools to East Anglia as underdogs.

Pools on this occasion were without Brian Honour, who was suspended, but they did have the big bustling Paul Baker up front. It was Paul who put Pools ahead, much to the delight of the away fans. Hartlepool held on to that lead almost until the final whistle, but Jason Dozell broke Pools fans' hearts with a goal just four minutes from time, making the final score 1-1.

However, Pools would have another crack at Ipswich and this time it would be in front of a crowd of enthusiastic Hartlepool United fans at The Vic.

Other news filtering through that weekend was that Wrexham, with the mercurial Mickey Thomas, had beaten Arsenal 2-1 in the Cup and Dennis Smith had been sacked by Sunderland.

Rob McKinnon was on his way to Scotland to join Motherwell for around £150,000. As Rob said at the time, "I'm not going to get picked for Scotland playing in Division Three." By joining the Fir Park team, Rob would realise his dream and play for his homeland not once, but three times.

It was a very cold 7th January 1992 when Hartlepool played Hull City in the Associate Members Cup and most of the supporters decided to stay at home and watch the telly. The lowest crowd for more than a year in the Auto Glass trophy saw Pools win. Brian was back from suspension. Pools took the lead when Olsson left Wayne Jacobs for dead. He went crackers.

Olsson passed to Paul Baker and Baker clipped it to Paul Dalton, who headed it home. Paul Olsson was born in Hull and showed the City fans what they had missed. Ten minutes before half-time, Paul tipped a short free kick to Baker, whose low shot found the bottom corner of the net. Pools were home and dry, if not freezing, with a 2-0 victory.

Before Hartlepool's game with Chester on 11th January, their manager Alan Murray received the Barclays Manager of the Month award. The mythical hoodoo associated with the award at the time seemed to be about that afternoon. It had been anticipated that Hartlepool would have an easy win over Chester, who were struggling at the time, but it was Pools who struggled to find the net and at half-time and it was all square at 0-0.

Eight minutes after the break, with the ball bobbing around in the Chester goalmouth, Baker's shot was blocked and the ball ran loose. Brian dashed in and from about 10 yards crashed the ball into the back of the City net. His celebration was almost as good as the goal.

Then, two minutes from time, Brian almost added a second. However, his cracking shot was tipped away by Chester keeper Stewart and the game ended in a disappointing 1-0 win, but a win nevertheless.

By the time the FA Cup third round replay against Ipswich came around, on 15th January, the town was buzzing. The draw had been made for the fourth round and if Pools could dispose of the 'Tractor Boys' they would face the winners of the Newcastle United versus Bournemouth tie. Brian had been relishing the thought of Pools playing the Magpies, but he would have to wait a few years yet to realise his dream.

Brian was back from suspension and 19-year-old Steve Fletcher would play for Pools. He would face the Ipswich Town captain, David Linighan (27), who returned 'home' to the Vic where he started his great career. One Ipswich striker could have missed the game due to a pending prison sentence. He had fallen foul of the law for a second drink-driving offence, but he was a lucky lad and escaped with a Community Service Order. Other high-profile drink drivers would not be so lucky, as Terry Fenwick, Tony Adams and the late great George Best could testify.

Ipswich flew into Teesside Airport, unlike Pools who went by coach for the first match. That was the difference between the top and the 'not so rich' in those days.

It could have all backfired on the Ipswich team, however, as a few miles up the road Newcastle Airport was closed. The replay between Newcastle United and Bournemouth fell victim to the fog after only 17 minutes with the score at 0-0. The fog on the Tyne was the only winner that night.

Back at the Victoria Ground, Jason Dozell, who had broken Hartlepool hearts in the first game with his last-ditch equaliser, scored for the second time. When a 20-yard rocket from Simon Milton hit the back of Pools' net the dream of a visit to St James Park was over. Paul Baker did think he had scored at one point, but as he turned to salute the home fans he saw the linesman's flag raised for offside.

Young Fletcher went close, too, as he stooped to head a cross from Brian Honour, but it was not to be.

Ipswich Town, led by a former Hartlepool player David Linighan, who went to school at English Martyrs, did a professional job and went back to East Anglia - by plane - to await the winners of the Magpies versus Cherries replay.

The crowd of 6,700 did have their money's worth, even if the result was not what they had hoped for.

Three days later, on 18th January, Pools were on the road again, this time to Lancashire to face Bolton Wanderers and another 6,000+ crowd. Pools had signed Paul Cross from Barnsley for £20,000 to replace Rob McKinnon, who had gone to Motherwell for £150,000. Cross was supposed to make his debut for Pools but inexplicably was left out of the side.

The game was only three minutes old when Brian Honour was brought down by David Burke. Brian took the free kick and floated it towards the teenager Fletcher at the far post.

Alan Stubbs made a hash of the clearance and gave away a corner. Brian, thinking quickly, played a one-two with Fletch and when Honour crossed the ball Olsson was there to head home his fifth goal of the season. Hartlepool United went in for a half-time cuppa leading 1-0.

Bolton came out all guns firing after the break and goals from Walker and Darley had the home fans singing. The game went into the last five minutes. Olsson, who was arguably the Man of the Match for Pools, closed down Kelly, who attempted a back pass to his goalkeeper. The totally mistimed ball sailed past the keeper and into the net, leading to a final score of 2-2: the great escape, with a little help from our friend Kelly at Bolton.

On 21st January Hartlepool played their third game in six days and the pace was beginning to take its toll on both the players and the fans' pockets. In less than a week the diehard, never-say-die Hartlepool fans had forked out hard-earned cash for the Ipswich game, the trip to Bolton and now this Associate Members Cup match against Scunthorpe. Understandably perhaps, only 1,361 turned up.

There was also bad news for one of Pools' sponsors - Cameron's Brewery. They had recently been taken over by Wolverhampton and Dudley Breweries and that month, as part of a 'rationalisation' programme, they announced 200 job losses at the Lion Brewery where Brian's brother John worked as a drayman. Such news always hits a town hard and this time it brought back memories for Brian of the lads on the dole during the long and bitter miners' dispute. Nobody wants to start the New Year by being told they have lost their job.

The strong-arm tactics of the Wolverhampton-based company were condemned by MP Ted Leadbitter. Ted had fought many battles on behalf of local people, and the fight to protect the jobs of the lads at the Lion Brewery would be one of his last. He retired in April 1992 and was replaced by Peter Mandelson, who later became Secretary for Northern Ireland in Blair's government before going on to become a European Commissioner. Mr Leadbitter sadly died following a road accident in December 1996.

Back at the Vic in the Members Cup, Scunthorpe had two 6 foot 3 strikers in Ian Helliwell and Jason White, who would cause the home side problems. But it was a defender who would have the first say in the game. Scunny's Stuart Hicks, in attempting to pass back to his goalkeeper, had not counted on the speed of little Brian Honour, who nipped in before the keeper could say "Gordon Banks" and slotted the ball past a bemused Phil Whitehead. But the Lincolnshire side bounced back and within five minutes equalised when Hamilton blazed home a great shot.

John Tinkler would hit Pools' winner on 74 minutes, but it was once again Brian Honour who stood out in so far as the press corps was concerned. They reported that in addition to scoring he had a powerful shot saved by Whitehead. Brian Honour was deemed "the most impressive player".

It looked for a long time as though the next fixture, on 1st February against Hull City, would fall foul of the weather which was, in a word, foul. The fog was rolling in off the Humber Estuary as Pools battled to beat City before 3,483 fans.

Paul Dalton knocked in the first goal after 20 minutes to give Pools a 1-0 lead at the interval. Paul Cross had made his long-awaited debut and on six minutes Brian Honour lobbed the ball over Shotton to Paul Dalton. The Hull man brought Dalton down with a crude tackle. Honour took the kick but it eluded everyone and a chance had passed. In the 54th minute, however, Paul Baker netted his sixteenth goal of the season to give Pools a two-goal advantage.

Although the thick fog held off enough for Pools to win 2-0, a 'red mist' had definitely descended on Hull manager, Terry Dolan, who was warned by the referee and told to get back in the dugout after venting his anger once to many times.

The tide turned somewhat in the Autoglass Trophy match on 4th February, however, when Beanpole Kevin Francis, standing 6 foot 7 in his stockinged feet, sent Pools crashing out with a hat-trick for Stockport County. Goals in the 14th, 50th and 72nd minutes would see United soundly beaten before a crowd of 2,255 fans. Brian Honour saw his 30-yard effort dip just too late to bother the keeper.

Pools did win 1-0 on bookings, though, as John Tinkler found his way into the ref's notebook for retaliation after he had been felled by a crunching tackle from Beaumont, of which his namesake, Bill, of Rugby Union fame, would have been proud.

It was a bad week, too, for Brian's favourite club, Newcastle United. They lost 5-2 to Oxford United and Ossie Ardilles was sacked to be replaced by Kevin Keegan.

Between New Year's Day and 4th February, Hartlepool United were required to play no fewer than eight games in less than 26 days, if you include a nine-day lay-off for the weather. The fixture congestion, however, would eventually cost Pools a possible promotion place.

In February Hartlepool played seven games in 29 days (Leap Year) and failed to score in five of them. They achieved a 2-0 win at Hull, in which Dalton and Baker scored, and a home win over Preston North End on 15th February, when Baker netted again and Jason Peake, who was on loan from Leicester City, also scored. Six points from a possible 21 saw Hartlepool drop from 7th to 13th in the League.

Things got even worse on 3rd March when, at home to Bolton Wanderers, Pools crashed 4-0. But three subsequent wins on the bounce that month, over Stockport, West Brom and Darlington, got the season back on track.

Hartlepool then faced a trip to Craven Cottage to take on Fulham, and the possibility of a double was on the cards. Fulham won 1-0, but Pools back home had two good wins against Shrewsbury and Exeter before returning to the capital to take on Leyton Orient. Again Hartlepool came unstuck in London, losing 4-0.

A draw with Stoke at home, when Olsson scored Pools' goal, was followed by a trip to St Andrews to face promotion hopefuls Birmingham City. Pools lost 2-1 with over 13,500 spectators at the ground.

After three lacklustre draws in April - at home to Bury 0-0 and away at Wigan and at Swansea - Pools finished the season on 2nd May with a home game against Bournemouth, in which Lenny Johnrose scored the only goal before 2,612 at the Vic.

Hartlepool lost nine games by the odd goal. Had the results of those matches been a draw, it may well have taken the team into the play-offs in a season when the 6th place club, Peterborough United, gained promotion via the play-offs.

The FA Cup run, the League Cup encounters and four games in the Members Cup had seen Hartlepool players take to the field on 58 occasions that season.

Martin Hodge, John McPhail and Brian Honour all clocked up 40 games each and only Paul Dalton, Keith Nobbs and Paul Olsson played more. Although the record books show that Pools used 29 players in the campaign when you discount those who only reached single figures, the main burden of a long, long season was shouldered by just 16 players.

In the end, the squad was simply too small to sustain a title challenge.

In the Palmer
of His Hand

Andy Saville was to feature quite prominently in 1992-93 and signalled his intentions before over 4,100 on the first game of the season at home to Brighton by slotting home his first penalty. The match ended in a 1-1 draw, and in all Andy would score seven times from the spot.

Three days later, on 18th August, United travelled to Halifax Town, and goals from John MacPhail and Lenny Johnrose in a 2-1 win in the first round, first leg of the League Cup made the journey home from Yorkshire quite enjoyable.

In the second leg Pools finished the job with two goals from Lenny and one from Southall, to set up a clash with their old friends from Sheffield Wednesday. More than 10,000 saw the away leg and Wednesday win 3-0, but when they travelled to Hartlepool it was a different story.

On 6th October Hartlepool United entertained Sheffield Wednesday in the second leg of the League Cup and, 3-0 up from their first encounter at Hillsborough, Wednesday arrived at Victoria Park in a buoyant mood.

Nowadays it's easy to criticise the modern-day footballer. Players of average ability earn obscene sums of cash as television continues to attract advertising and subscription dollars from around the globe. Players are frequently caught with lap dancers, they plough their sports cars into innocent bystanders, they piss in plant pots in front of Americans only days after 9/11, groupies are 'roasted', £20 notes are used to light cigars, supporters are kicked, punched and spat on, thousands of pounds are gambled on horse races they don't even watch, drug tests are 'forgotten about', and the average fan is treated with utter contempt by a sickening few. Grown men, who should be privileged to earn a living playing the game they love, behave disgracefully week in, week out.

And with the above in mind, I can guarantee you that nothing could give you a more prophetic indication of where the game was heading than what happened at Victoria Park in 1992.

The game itself finished 2-2, meaning that United went out 5-2 on aggregate, but for once the football was not the issue. Lining up for Wednesday that night was Carlton Lloyd Palmer. Palmer would finish his career with 18 England caps, scoring one goal. But, to be blunt, his brief spell wearing the 3 lions coincided with one of the most forgettable periods in the history of our nation's sport. A personification of everything wrong with the 'Graham Taylor era', Palmer was picked for industry, drive and work rate, ahead of guile, craft and skill.

During the game Palmer said to Brian, "What were you doing during the summer? I was playing for England!"

Given that Palmer was referring to the 1992 European Championships in which England finished bottom of their group and only scored one goal in the whole tournament, it seemed like a bizarre thing to be boasting about!

Brain, bemused, responded politely, "I went to Salou with my wife."

The game continued and Brian jinked his way into the penalty area only to be clattered from behind by the gangly Palmer.

Penalty!

"You cheating little bastard!" screamed the Wednesday man.

"Fuck off!" replied Honour.

The two had to be pulled apart by teammates.

Andy Saville scored the resulting spot kick, but for the rest of the game Brian would suffer a torrent of abuse from the England man.

"How many cars have you got?" asked Palmer as they jockeyed for position at a corner.

"How many houses have you got?" he continued as Brian picked the ball up for a throw-in.

"How many England caps have you got?"

"How much money have you got in the bank?"

The torrent of unnecessary abuse continued throughout the game.

Even Palmer's own teammates Chris Waddle, Danny Wilson and Nigel Worthington were disgusted with what they saw.

"Shut up, Carlton", "Leave it", "Don't be a prick" are just some of the comments attributed to the more mature Wednesday players lining up with Palmer that night.

Brian himself, other that his retort on being called a "Cheating little bastard", maintained a dignified silence and refused to bite.

There's an old Chinese saying: "If you wait by the river long enough, eventually you'll see the bodies of your enemies float by." And nothing could be truer in football.

Several years later Palmer would go on to manage Mansfield Town and Stockport County. At Mansfield he would win just 10 of his 41 games in charge before being dismissed. At Stockport he lost 50 of his 92-game tenure before throwing in the towel. Carlton Palmer may have stood at 6 foot 3 inches tall, but as he lurched down the tunnel at Victoria Park that night in 1992 it was Brian Honour who left the pitch the bigger man.

For the football purists, the Pools scorers were Lenny Johnrose and Saville from the spot.

Meanwhile, back in the League in August, Hartlepool were unbeaten with a draw at Rotherham United and a 1-0 win at home over Huddersfield Town, with Olsson netting the winner.

September started with a home win over Chester, with Ryan Cross and Dean Emerson on the score sheet. It was to be Emerson's only goal in 32 starts for Pool, but he is perhaps best remembered for the five yellow cards he picked up that season.

On 5th September the long trip south to Bournemouth at last brought some joy after some miserable performances at Dean Court. Cross was on target again and Andy Saville scored from open play to take Pools into 3rd place. Hartlepool kept that 3rd spot the next week with a good 2-2 draw at Wigan, both goals coming again from Saville. Wigan Athletic would be relegated in May.

A reverse at home to Leyton Orient saw Pools slump 2-0 and drop five places in the League. But Olsson scored in the next home game for a 1-1 draw with Port Vale. Vale would make the play-offs but go no further.

On the road again, at Preston North End, Lenny Johnrose scored as did John Gallacher. It was to be his only goal in 16 starts but it gave Pools a very good 2-0 win at Deepdale.

An Andy Saville penalty on 2nd October at home to Blackpool before just 2,675 was enough for Pools to win 1-0 and go into 2nd place. And Saville was again on the mark at Bolton Wanderers the following week, supported by Lenny Johnrose, in a 2-1 win to keep Pools in the runners-up spot.

However, as so often happens back at the Victoria Ground, whilst pulling in the largest crowd of the season so far at 4,396, Pools lost 1-0 to Swansea City. The Swans would make the play-offs but go no further.

Another long trip to the south coast saw Brian Honour get on the score sheet in a 1-1 draw with Brighton, and the following week more than 4,300 turned up again at home to Bradford City. There were no slip-ups this time, with Southall and Paul Wratten scoring in the 2-0 win. Wratten, who was previously with Manchester United, would turn out just ten times this season and that was his only goal - but a valuable one as Hartlepool rose to 3rd from top.

November started as bleak as it could get with two 3-1 defeats, away to West Brom before 13,000 and at home to Exeter City. The Baggies were promoted via the play-offs and Exeter missed the drop by just four points. But their turn would come.

The twin strike force of Saville and Johnrose hit the net again with a goal from Ian McGuckin, who was on loan from Fulham. Pools beat Stockport County on 28th November 3-2.

In the cold light of day, this was a side that on form could beat any in the Division. On a miserable December day the team went south again to Plymouth and Johnrose and Saville ensured that Pools had a share of the spoils in a 2-2 draw with Argyle. Then on 8th December, in the Associate Members Cup, just 1,193 fans saw Hartlepool demolish Scarborough 4-1 at the Victoria Ground with goals from Olsson, Johnson, Saville and Brian Honour.

If only they could have scored those goals in the League!

Back home on the worst Saturday of the season, when many men were dragged off Christmas shopping, the Hartlepool fan base held firm with 4,136 in the Vic for the home game with Stoke City. Brian Honour scored for Pools, but City hit back and went away with all three points. The team went into the Christmas break in 9th position.

Boxing Day, as always, provided some good news for United. More than 4,230 attended the game stuffed full of turkey and the team were handed a belated Christmas present from Hull City with Lenny Johnrose netting again.

The final League game of the old year on 28th December was away to Fulham. Andy Saville netted two, one from the spot, and Nicky Southall the other in a great 3-1 away win. That put Pools in 4th spot and was just where the fans wanted to be on New Year's Eve - in a play-off place.

The Palace Dethroned at United

In the FA Cup Pools knocked out Doncaster Rovers on their own turf on 14th November 1992, with a goal from Johnrose and Andy Saville's customary penalty. Then, on 6th December, at home to Southport, Andy Saville proved what a quality striker he was, scoring a hat-trick as Pools ran out easy winners 4-0, the fourth goal coming from Nicky Peverell.

The first fixture of the New Year, on 2nd January 1993, saw Crystal Palace visit Hartlepool in a third round FA Cup game. Palace were playing in the top tier of English football at the time; in fact, it was only three short seasons since the Eagles had almost won the famous old trophy, losing in a replay against the mighty Manchester United. (A cup run that apparently saved one Sir Alex Ferguson from the sack!)

With Britain's first million-pound goalkeeper in Nigel Martyn between the sticks, together with a host of internationals including Geoff Thomas, Chris Armstrong, Chris Coleman and Eddie McGoldrick in Palace's line-up, it was a classic 'David versus Goliath' encounter. However, like the biblical battle, the winner was far from a foregone conclusion.

Pools survived wave after wave of Palace attacks and held firm with a solid defence, helped by Chris Armstrong, who had one of those games where he couldn't have hit a cow's arse with a banjo. Late in the game came what was practically Pools' only chance of the match.

Nicky Southall jinked into the penalty area and was challenged from behind by Richard Shaw. Even the most diehard Poolie would admit that contact was 'minimal', but in the 84th minute, with the score at 0-0, Southall did what any self-respecting forward would do in the same situation - he went down like he'd been shot in the head.

To say that he'd dived would be unkind, but the fact that he was a stone's throw away from the two-metre springboard at the Mill House swimming baths is perhaps appropriate. This was poetry. He didn't just go down, he did it with style, grace and finesse. All that was missing was a tuck or a pike and a score of 5.8 for artistic impression. Best of all, the referee bought it … PENALTY!

Andy Saville held his nerve and slotted the ball home from the spot, and the third round 'coupon buster' was on. Pools held on for the final few minutes to claim the scalp and the headlines on *Match of the Day* that evening.

Palace and their fans made the long trek back to London dejected and feeling hard done by. Pools and the blue and white army didn't care. This was their day in the sunshine and the fourth round would see them travel to Sheffield United and Alan Cork's beard!

There are some fans who believe that the Cup run that season cost Hartlepool United a play-off place at least.

However, on 23rd January the Hartlepool fans had another great away day, this time in Sheffield at Bramall Lane facing United. More than 20,000 packed the terraces that day, including a loud contingent from Hartlepool. Pools lost 1-0 to Sheffield United, who would go on to the semi-final held on 3rd April 1993 where they would meet near neighbours Sheffield Wednesday at Wembley Stadium. The Wednesday team contained Chris Waddle, Mark Bright and the obnoxious Carlton Palmer and they were favourites to beat United.

More than 75,000 travelled south to see who would earn a place in the FA Cup final and secure bragging rights for the rest of the year.

Waddle delivered an early blow for the Owls with one of his trademark free kicks. However, the Blades were undeterred and, vowing not to shave until United had lost in the Cup, the bearded veteran striker Alan Cork, looking like something out of a caveman movie, popped up with a goal to take the semi-final into extra time.

The atmosphere at Wembley was electric, and when Mark Bright tapped in the winner to send the blue and whites into ecstasy United suffered immediate depression.

Mrs Cork would have her wish. Alan would have to shave.

Sheffield Wednesday would go on to meet Arsenal in the FA Cup final. Hartlepool fans on that day were firmly behind The Gunners, as Carlton Palmer's disgraceful behaviour lingered in their memories, and they would have the last laugh as a former Hartlepool player would score the winner.

The first game on 15th May ended all square, with Ian Wright scoring for Arsenal and David Hirst equalising. George Graham was the Arsenal boss and Tony Adams the captain. At number five was the former English Martyrs pupil who plied his trade at Hartlepool United, Andy Linighan. Trevor Francis was the Wednesday manager, with Viv Anderson leading the side.

The replay took place at Wembley on 20th May. More than 141,000 fans watched both games at the stadium and millions more from around the world tuned into the BBC's *Match of the Day* programme.

Viv Anderson was missing from the Sheffield team due to injury and the obnoxious Mr Palmer took over as captain. Danny Wilson, who was later to become Hartlepool United's manager, played for an hour before being substituted. The change had an almost immediate effect, with Chris Waddle scoring to cancel out Ian Wright's 34th-minute goal.

Keren Barratt, the referee, blew the whistle to signal another period of extra time and on 119 minutes, with the tie looking deadlocked, the lad from Hartlepool United who had played 130 games for his home town club between 1981 and 1984 forced the ball home.

Arsenal won the FA Cup 2-1 and Carlton Palmer was silent - for once! Revenge is oh so sweet!

In the League, from 9th January until 6th March Pools would fail to score in 11 consecutive games - more than 1,200 minutes of football. As a result, the team dropped from 4th to 16th place, and by the time Wigan Athletic visited Hartlepool on 2nd March the crowds too had fallen from almost 4,500 to a meagre 1,791.

The goal drought was eventually broken on 6th March at Blackpool when Andy Saville scored from open play, but with just 13 games remaining the drought had cost Pools dearly.

The crowds did return momentarily on 9th March when Burnley were the visitors, but the match ended 0-0. This was followed by a long, fruitless trip to Exeter on 13th March, when the only consolation was a goal from Mick Tait, his only one that season, as Pools went down 3-1.

Promotion hopefuls West Brom were the next visitors, and two goals from Andy Saville in the 2-2 draw perhaps gave a further indication as to what might have been. On 23rd March Andy Saville would play his final game for Hartlepool United. They had lost a striker of tremendous ability.

Three defeats on the bounce to Stockport 4-1, Mansfield at home 1-0 and Burnley away 3-0 saw Pools drop to 19th position in the League. The slide was reflected in the crowd on 5th April, when only 1,822 arrived at the Vic. They were to miss a Brian Honour goal as Plymouth Argyle were beaten 1-0. But after that the slide continued, with defeats at Fulham and Hull City.

Lenny Johnrose stopped the rot on 17th April, when Hartlepool United beat Stoke City 1-0 away before 17,331 fans. Stoke would be promoted in May as League Champions and Hartlepool would finish in 16th place.

A 3-0 defeat at Swansea perhaps indicated what a topsy-turvy season this was all round, with possibly any one team from the top 12 capable of achieving promotion. Swansea reached the play-offs, but it was West Brom who would go up.

Hartlepool United had beaten champions Stoke City and runners-up Bolton Wanderers, both on their own grounds, and had drawn with the third promoted club West Brom. So where did it all go wrong?

The eleven-match run when Pools could not buy a goal was the obvious answer. But that was little consolation for the fans who watched the two final games of the season, as Hartlepool beat Brighton at the Vic 2-0 and Bradford City away by the same score.

In the closed season Andy Saville would go, as would Lenny Johnrose after just nine games and also Peverell. The burden of scoring would fall on the old warhorse Houchen, who would trot out for 34 games, scoring eight goals. It would prove a bridge too far for Keith.

Brian Honour would play just 17 starts, plus subs, scoring three goals.

Relegation!

Hartlepool made the worst possible start to the 1993-94 season, going down at home to Fulham who would be relegated come the next May. A crowd of just over 2,500 saw the game. Home attendances would drop as low as 1,077, which was perhaps the fans' reaction to the 'family silver', in the guise of a great many of the best players, being sold off.

In the first round of the League Cup, sponsored by Coca Cola, West scored a goal to level matters at Stockport to give Hartlepool a fighting chance in the second leg at home.

Before that match a visit to Brighton yielded a point with a Gallacher goal in a 1-1 draw.

The Coca Cola Cup first round, second leg match was played on 24th August 1993, and to say that Brian Honour could not have picked a better time to score this match winning goal would be an understatement.

Pool were a goal down with two minutes of injury time already played when Mick Tait put the home side level to make it 2-2 on aggregate. The tie looked destined for extra time until a long clearance was headed on by Ian McGuckin to Brian, who easily disposed of his marker to send a screaming 40-yard volley into the net to snatch an incredible win. The victory set Pool up with a second round tie against Sheffield Wednesday.

Middlesbrough-born McGuckin began life as a trainee with Pools and stayed for six seasons before moving to Fulham. He also played with Oxford United and Barrow and ended his playing days with Durham City in the Northern League.

On 28th August Pools were at home to Bournemouth and Brian scored in another 1-1 draw. Three days later, on the road at Leyton Orient, Hartlepool scored a rare away win that season when West again was on target, supported by Southall, to clinch a 2-1 win. Pools moved up to 13th place.

September started as August, with a defeat, this time away to Exeter. Southall scored a consolation for Pools, but as Exeter would be relegated at the end of the season the writing was on the wall and the leaves had not started to fall off the trees.

Back at the Vic, Thompson scored the only goal against Stockport, which was followed by another home win, 2-0, on 14th September against Blackpool, with West netting his third goal of the season supported by one from Brian. Only 2,124 attended the game. As a result, Hartlepool United moved up to 8th from top - the highest position they would occupy that season.

On 18th September a visit to the Potteries and the home of Sir Stanley Matthews, the man who had visited little Brian all those years earlier, would not repeat the joy the little four-year-old had experienced at that time. Pools went down 1-0 and Vale would go on to finish runners-up and gain promotion.

The significant feature of that match, however, was that playing in the number 7 shirt was the former Boro legend, Bernie 'Wolfman' Slaven. In December I caught up with the Wolfman at the Tall Trees Motel, near Yarm, and discussed the game played all those years earlier. Bernie remembered Brian vividly and also Pools centre half on the day, John McPhail. The latter and Bernie exchanged several tackles that day.

Bernie of course played with distinction at Albion Rovers, Middlesbrough and Port Vale and also in one season, which was a big mistake, at Darlington. But Brian Honour and Bernie 'Wolfman' Slaven did face each other on the pitch at Port Vale and many years later they would meet again in less hostile surroundings.

Bernie Slaven is a legend in the north-east and is part of the 'Three Legends', a radio show broadcast every weekday evening in the region. His two pals on the show are Malcolm McDonald of Newcastle United and Mick Horswill, late of Sunderland. Mick replaced Eric Gates.

In his seven-and-a-half years at Middlesbrough Bernie experienced the high and lows that this north-east club had to offer. When it was time to move on, he was approached by several clubs. His former boss at Boro, Bruce Rioch, who was in charge at Bolton, Ossie Ardilles at West Brom and Forest were all thought to be interested in capturing his signature. After all, he was a proven goalscorer.

In the event, the unlikely winners in the race for Slaven's signature were Potteries club Port Vale. They were they only club that offered a longer contract - longer, that is, than the end of the season.

Port Vale would reach the play-offs in his first season, 1992-93, but first they had an appearance at Wembley on 22nd May 1993 when they picked up the Auto Glass Trophy, beating Stockport County 2-1. They also beat County by the same score to reach Wembley again in the play-offs, but this time they lost 3-0 to West Bromwich Albion.

Port Vale were promoted in the 1993-94 season as runners-up. Bernie's contribution was 9 goals in 33 appearances. Once again he had delivered the goods.

Also in that season they were drawn at home to the then top-flight Southampton and Port Vale ran out winners 1-0: a Premiership scalp for the underdogs. They drew Wolves in the next round and lost 2-0.

Bernie then moved to Darlington, where 37 appearances would yield seven goals. He then moved on to become a 'legend' on the radio and produced several books via the publishing company he formed with broadcaster Alistair Brownlee.

Brian and Bernie shared memories of that day when Port Vale beat Pools 1-0. Bernie described Brian as "a great guy", and that really says it all.

Anyway, back to Pools. The League Cup was supposed to provide some relief but a 3-0 defeat away to Grimsby Town in the first leg and a 2-0 defeat at home were typical of the season. The crowd was down to 1,385.

However, worse was to come on 25th September when York City visited the Vic. The Bootham Crescent mob came in numbers and the attendance went up to 3,050, which would only be surpassed on the traditional Boxing Day fixture. York won 2-0 and they would finish in a play-off place.

Brian scored against his old club Darlington on 28th September when the Quakers visited the Vic in the Associate Members Cup, but the crowd would only include the hardy, never-say-die Pools fans - all 1,454 of them.

October saw more defeats: 2-0 at Burnley, who would go up via the play-offs; 1-0 at home to Brentford; away at Cambridge by the same score; and at home to Bradford 2-1, with Johnrose scoring Pools' consolation goal.

That amounted to six defeats on the bounce with only one goal to show for 540 minutes of less than breathtaking football.

Johnrose was on target again on 30th October at Cardiff and somehow, with a goal from West, Hartlepool came away with a point. However, that was one point from a possible 21 points - hardly promotion form, in fact quite the opposite.

With the start of a new month, November brought a ray of hope as Pools beat Barnet at the Vic 2-1 with goals from Keith Houchen and Johnrose again. Less than 2,000 turned up. Did they know that Barnet would finish holding up the rest of the League with only one away win all season? Thankfully it wasn't at Pools.

On 6th November West scored again, this time away to Bristol Rovers in a creditable 1-1 draw. Rovers would miss out on the play-offs by just three points, and more than 5,200 saw this game as a clear indication of the difference between success and failure.

A 2-0 away defeat to York on 9th November meant that Pools could concentrate on the League, but in the interim there was the small matter of a first round FA Cup match at Macclesfield. Pools lost 2-0 and there would be no Cup run this season.

Back at home on 17th November, Wrexham were the visitors and although Southall scored for Pools the team lost again 2-1 before 1,530. A long trip to Plymouth on 27th November reaped another 2-0 defeat. Plymouth would reach the play-offs but fall at the final hurdle.

Their performance in the League was going from bad to worse. November, which had started so brightly with the win against Barnet, would yield only four points from a possible 12.

Following the Plymouth defeat, Lenny Johnrose would not play for Pools again and he eventually joined Bury. Having lost Andy Saville and Johnrose, where would the goals come from? Well, the old warhorse Houchen had returned and he would chip in eight goals from 34 starts.

A seaside trip to Blackpool on 4th December saw Pools lose 2-1 and they couldn't even score - the goal was credited to a player in tangerine as an own goal.

Pools had scored just 15 goals all season and Blackpool's Andy Watson had scored that number himself.

On 1st December Gary Gibson, the Pools chairman, decided to make cutbacks to save £300,000. He cut the wages bill: Dean Emerson went to Stockport County, Paul Cross to Darlo and Paul Olsson looked set to join the Quakers too. Alan Murray was then in charge at Feethams and he knew all about the Pools players. The taxman was taking Pools to the High Court and a bleak winter saw both Viv Busby and Eric Gates leave. John Gallacher, believed to be the highest-paid player on the books, was talking with the club to try to buy out his contract. The only bright spot was that Nicky Southall decided to stay. But where did all the money go from the sale of the 'family silver'? That was the question on many fans' lips.

On 9th December a former member of the 1990 promotion squad, Ricardo Gabbiadini, moved to the Irish League side Linfield, and Danny Blanchflower, an Irish legend, died after a long illness.

Pools Players Go on Strike!

On 10th December problems for MacPhail, the Pools boss, mounted, as the entire first team went on strike when their pay cheques bounced. The following day the players called off the strike, but it was not the preparation the team needed for the game with Brighton.

In those dark, dark days of winter 1993, one bright spot was the home game with Brighton and Hove Albion on 11th December. Southall put Pools in front after 15 minutes. McGuckin was dismissed after two yellow cards and Codner's ferocious strike levelled it at 1-1. On 83 minutes Brian Honour scored from the spot, but with just 60 seconds on the clock Nicky Bissett levelled it for Brighton and the game ended 2-2. Fans showed their disgust by booing and jeering Hartlepool's chairman, Gary Gibson.

On 14th December Pools players went on strike again after their pay cheques bounced for a second time. They had only received a percentage of the monies due to them and the PFA intervened to talk to the club.

On the road again, on the Saturday that wives traditionally used to drag their husbands off to do the Christmas shopping, Pools were at Fulham and any wives who made the trip to London could buy their gifts in the West End. Not, I suspect, that many had any win bonuses to spend. And they wouldn't have one from this game either, as Fulham won 2-0 to complete a double over Pools. In May, however, Fulham would be relegated! Colin West was one of the few players to emerge with any credit. No doubt the Fulham players got paid on time and their last pay day before Christmas was not clouded by a bounced cheque.

The decision by Gibson to offload players left Pools well short of experience. Denny Ingram, aged just 17 years, was the first choice as right back. That said it all.

On 21st December Pools faced the possibility of having to play behind closed doors because of delays in the improvements at the Vic. The current safety certificate was due to run out on 31st December 1993. On top of that, four players were hit by the flu, including Colin West and Brian.

On 27th December the traditional Boxing Day fixture was held and the crowd went up to 3,286 for Huddersfield Town's visit. Pools' goal was scored from the spot by Southall. That was to be the only bright spot for the Hartlepool faithful, as the side from West Yorkshire ran out easy winners 4-1. There was no message of seasonal comfort for the suffering fans and it is to their credit that so many turned out for the game. Keith Houchen was sent off as the ref lost control and Colin West, MacPhail, Tait and Southall all went into the referee's bulging book, along with two Huddersfield players. Houchen was sent off for allegedly swearing at the linesman, an offence he denies to this day.

After the match Brian was diagnosed with a twisted knee and was ruled out of the scheduled match with Hull City, which rounded off the old year with a 1-0 away defeat.

Pools had slumped to 23rd in the League, and Brian Honour would say good riddance to 1993 - a roller-coaster ride that had seen financial problems, unpaid wages, an FA Cup win over Crystal Palace and the club sink to its lowest ebb for years. It had been a thoroughly miserable year and surely 1994 would bring better fortune for the fans at the Victoria Ground.

Brian was quite philosophical at the time, however: "I have been at Hartlepool for nine-and-a-half years. What has happened this year is sad, so very sad. But there's only one thing we can do. We roll our sleeves up and get ourselves out of this mess." He added, "It's hard to prepare for games when so much is happening off the field, but we should forget about it and concentrate on the game."

The New Year started with new hope when on New Year's

Day Rotherham visited Pools. Two goals from Keith Houchen at least showed that he had lost none of the old touches that had brought him success in the FA Cup final with Coventry. In the final with Tottenham Hotspur, winning 2-1, Keith Houchen popped up to head home a superb equalising goal to take the final into extra time. A wicked shot in the extra half hour took a deflection off Gary Mabbutt's leg and looped into the Spurs net. Coventry won the FA Cup at Wembley, but the final will always be remembered for Houchen's superb diving header - and he was now at Hartlepool.

However, that was back in 1987, so could the old warhorse do it again several years later? Could Houchen single-handedly save Hartlepool from the drop?

The answer came a few days later away to Reading, the eventual League Champions, when Pools went down 4-0. The next home game with Cambridge United produced another defeat 2-0, followed by another at Brentford 1-0, before a goal from Thompson at Swansea gave Pools a point. Thompson scored again at Bradford before more than 7,900 fans but Pools lost 2-1.

Reading travelled north for the return fixture and again scored four goals, Pools going down 4-1. McGuckin scored the consolation effort. Another long trip to Bournemouth saw Pools keep a clean sheet, the first in the League since 14th September, picking up a rare point on the road in a 0-0 draw.

McGuckin scored again at home to Exeter on 26th February, but Pools lost 2-1. No clean sheet in this game and only two more in the rest of the season.

If the alarm bells weren't already ringing they should be now.

Another away day saw Pools cross the Pennines for the game with Stockport County, where they lost 5-0. Then it was back to the Vic on 8th March, the crowd down to 1,251. These were dark times, but Southall brightened the day with a goal. However, Leyton Orient went back to London with a point in the 1-1 draw.

Port Vale, who would consolidate their runners-up spot,

visited the Vic and tore the Pools defence to shreds. They scored four times with the only reply coming from MacPhail.

The defence leaked another three goals away to York City on 19th March without reply, and when Pools came to run out onto the pitch on 22nd March for the home game with Cardiff City only 1,077 fans were in attendance. It must be assumed that theses diehard folk were truly Hartlepool's greatest fans - and they deserved a medal. What they got for their loyalty was a rare 3-0 win, with Olsson, Southall from the spot and Keith Houchen scoring.

Could this rare form save Pools from the drop with just nine games to go?

When Burnley, who would be promoted through the play-offs, came visiting, the crowd was swelled by the Lancashire clubs supporters to 2,879. No one expected anything other than a Hartlepool defeat, but that great guy Keith Houchen popped up with two goals, supported by Southall and Thompson. Hartlepool United beat promotion candidates Burnley 4-1.

When the team went to Wales on 29th March to face Swansea City and Houchen scored again in a 1-0, optimism rose in the town, and when Pools picked up a point at Huddersfield in a 1-1 draw, with West on the score sheet, things looked a great deal brighter. Town had thrashed Pools 4-1 at the Vic in the festive season fixture and now Pools had held them at Leeds Road.

But football is a team game and Hartlepool United could not rely on the ageing Houchen, who was entering the twilight of his career. At home to Hull City on 4th April Pools lost 1-0. But five days later, on a trip to South Yorkshire, hopes were high of a rare double, as Pools had beaten Rotherham earlier in the season with two Houchen goals. It was not to be and Pools lost 7-0.

The bubble had definitely burst and would never be reinflated, well not that season in any event.

However, back home old Houchen did the business again when Bristol Rovers were the visitors, supported by a goal from Peverell in a 2-1 win. Olsson and Southall scored when Pools visited bottom club Barnet on 26th April, but Pools lost to the worst team in the League 3-2.

An expected 2-0 away defeat at Wrexham was followed by the final game of the season at the Vic, when Plymouth Argyle were the visitors. Hartlepool's management made it an all-ticket game, but only 2,382 turned up to watch the last game before relegation. The chairman had made a mistake in selling off the 'family silver' and he made another with this all-ticket farce.

Peverell scored a consolation goal for the home side, but Argyle ran in eight goals to finish their season in 3rd position with a play-off place. Two of Argyle's goals were scored by old Pools favourite Paul Dalton and his colleague Langdon hit a hat-trick. The 8-1 thrashing was to be Nicky Peverell's last game and he left the club. Argyle would not go up, however, as that honour went to Burnley.

Hartlepool United's defence had leaked 87 goals, with the forwards netting just 41 goals in 46 games. The home fans had seen their side beaten at home on a dozen occasions, conceding 40 goals at the Victoria Ground in 23 home games. They were relegated with Barnet, Fulham and Exeter City and it would be nine long years before they achieved promotion.

Brian Honour played only a bit part in the season, and those 14 or so operations on his knee, the back injury and all the other niggling injuries were taking their toll.

The little fella faced his worst nightmare - not playing football again.

He had been warned repeatedly by the medical people that his knee and leg injuries could cripple him in later life. But, as playing football was all he had ever wanted to do, Brian Honour played on.

Those of us who saw him play know what a battler he was. How many times through pain had he helped Hartlepool United to victory and in one glorious season to promotion?

Hartlepool did have a team that would reach a national Cup final that miserable May.

The Lion Hotel would meet Ranelagh Sports in the All England Sunday Cup final at Woking. Although Lion, managed by Bobby Brown, whose son Michael would grace the Premier League in later years, lost 2-0 in a tightly fought contest, they put up an excellent fight, despite some dodgy refereeing decisions. Lion Hotel would later be awarded the Hartlepool Sports Council's Outstanding Team Performance Award, a reward justly deserved.

In 1994 Brian Honour would play just one more game for Hartlepool United in the League in the 2-0 defeat at Bury on 16th August. The knee injury suffered in the Coca-Cola match with Bury was to end his career.

At the time I was selling football nets made by inmates at Durham Jail and Pools bought a set woven in blue and white. But the goal nets also would appear later that year at Wembley Stadium complete with the cross of St George, and at Hampden Park with the comparative cross of St Andrew.

Brian was forced to contemplate his future.

His loyal fans would have to wait almost a year before they could pay their final tribute to the little guy who had brought so much pleasure to the fans during his ten or so years with United. But when they did show their appreciation, the crowds were a lot larger than the lowest crowd of the 1993-94 season - just 1,077.

On 21st September Hartlepool were drawn in the League Cup against mighty Arsenal, who at that time were holders of the European Cup Winners Cup. In their team Arsenal fielded David Seaman in goal, plus eight other internationals and former Hartlepool United favourite Andy Linighan. Tony Adams opened the scoring, Ian Wright added a couple, and then Smith and Paul Merson made it 5-0. Only 4,421 turned up, including Brian who was a reluctant spectator.

For the return on 3rd October, 20,250 attended Highbury to see Arsenal run out winners on aggregate 7-0. Kevin Campbell, Paul Dickov, Ray Parlour and Seaman all featured in a Gunners team. George Graham was happy to win, as winning was all that mattered.

Sadly, Brian Honour would never pull on a Pools shirt in anger again. His next match would be in 1995 - his testimonial.

Gibson Out!

In May 1994 the anti Gary Gibson feeling was evident in the town. However, a saviour was waiting in the wings in the person of local millionaire, Mr Harold Hornsey, who expressed an interest in buying the club, but it was too late to save the club from going down.

Gibson hung on as long as he could to squeeze as much as he could out of the deal. Five more Hartlepool players were shown the door when the retained list was announced. Mick Tait had perhaps been an obvious candidate at 37 years of age and with more than 650 games under his belt. Paul Wratten and Nicky Peverell were also released. The biggest surprise, however, was that Pools let Paul Olsson go. He was the second longest-serving player behind Brian Honour.

Yes, 13th May was unlucky for those five players.

On 19th May Ian McGuckin rejected a new deal from Pools and they responded by placing a £500,000 price tag on his head. Even though he was Hartlepool's Player of the Year, it was a ridiculous price for a player relegated along with his teammates. But then, in the opinion of many Pools fans, Gary Gibson was renowned for making ridiculous decisions in so far as running the club was concerned. Or should that be 'ruining' the club?

On 24th May the good news that all Pools fans had been waiting for was announced in the *Hartlepool Mail*: Gary Gibson would go if Harold Hornsey wanted to buy Pools. The good news was short-lived, however, when two days later the deal collapsed. Mr Gibson, who had originally agreed a price thought to be in the region of £160,000, suddenly hiked up it up, allegedly, to £220,000.

The deal was on the verge of collapse and Hartlepool MP Ted Leadbitter intervened.

Finally, on 30th May 1994, Mr Harold Hornsey was able to announce that he had taken control of the club. In so doing, Hartlepool United were saved from the clutches of the Official Receiver and the Inland Revenue. The Hartlepool fans would be ever grateful to Mr Hornsey.

The Finale:
Brian's Testimonial

The testimonial match in 1995 was a culmination of Brian's testimonial year, granted by the club for 11 years with Hartlepool United. Malcolm Lancaster Testimonial Committee Chairman writes in the testimonial brochure:

"On behalf of the Brian Honour Testimonial Committee I would like to thank everyone who has supported our ventures this year.

"A special thanks, of course, goes to Kevin Keegan and his Newcastle players for agreeing to play in the testimonial game.

"Brian Honour has never hidden the fact that he has been a Newcastle fan since he was a child, and throughout his career has never missed an opportunity to stand on the St James Park terraces to watch the Magpies - even in the bad times.

"The fact that the club is now doing well and has regained its rightful place amongst the country's elite has thrilled Brian more than it has thrilled other football fans in the region.

"By agreeing to play this game and by bringing some of the country's best players to Hartlepool, Kevin Keegan has shown that he and his club have not grown too big that they can't remember their roots. Players like Brian Honour are what professional football is all about, and thanks to Newcastle United coming to Hartlepool, we can all recognise that fact.

"The other club we must thank is Hartlepool United for allowing us to stage the game.

"We are grateful to the many individuals and companies throughout the area who have helped us. We have asked a lot of people for a lot of help, and it is an illustration of the esteem in which people hold Brian that we have hardly ever been refused.

"Thanks to everyone who has helped and to everyone who paid to watch the Newcastle game.

"But most of all, thanks for the memories Brian."

Brian Honour's testimonial year ended on a high with a match against his beloved Newcastle United. Brian said his own farewells in a contribution simply called 'The Final Whistle':

"When I first started in professional football as a kid from the collieries, I never dreamed that one day I would be writing a column in a programme for my testimonial match.

"But the day is here ... my professional career is over and this is a 'big goodbye' for me as a player.

"I was very sad the day doctors told me I would have to pack in playing League football and over the last few months I have been coming to terms with the situation. But I think I can honestly say that there will be a big lump in my throat today, before, during and after the match.

"My only regret is that my dad John was not around when I turned professional.

"Although my career ended because of injury, I have to say I have a lot to be thankful for. I have had a tremendous career with Hartlepool United and have met and made good friends with a lot of very special people at the club ... players, staff, volunteer helpers and directors.

"I am proud to say that I have also made a lot of friends with the club's supporters and I will always regard my relationship with the fans as really something special.

"Nowadays we read a lot about players becoming millionaires, about huge transfer fees and lucrative moves to big foreign clubs.

"But you can't bank what I have managed from football, a lot of wonderful memories, a lot of wonderful friends and a lot of help from a lot of people.

"I can't really thank everybody individually, but I have to

thank the members of the Testimonial Committee through its chairman Malcolm Lancaster for their hard work in making today's match and a lot of other events very successful.

"Thanks also to all the players who are turning out today, my old colleagues from Hartlepool United and my heroes from Newcastle United.

"As I said earlier, as a teenager I never dreamed that one day there would be a testimonial game for me. If somebody had told me Newcastle United would be playing in it, I would have told them they were dreaming.

"But football can make dreams come true. It proved that to me many times.

"My thanks are also due to the officials of Hartlepool United for their help today and over the years.

"Last but by no means least a big thank you to all the people who have got behind me and the team over my years at the club. I will never forget the support I have had from the terraces during my career.

"Hartlepool United may not be the biggest club in the country and it certainly isn't the best supported, but to me the fans will always be the best.

"Thank you all".

Many testimonial tributes were made to Brian Honour from the footballing world, the media and, of course, his wife.

Rob McKinnon, Motherwell and Scotland:
"As a winger there was no one better and as a friend there is no one better. I was lucky to play behind Brian, because I would have hated to have marked him. The only time I remember playing against him, he broke my cheek bone in a pre-season practice match! He was a superb winger, both equally good at going outside a defender down the flank or cutting inside. And, unlike most wingers, he would track back and help his defence out with good marking and tackling. In fact, he was the most complete player. He would always give 100%. Brian is a great friend to myself and my wife

Bernadette and we are godparents to his lovely daughters. He deserves his big game for ten loyal years' service to Hartlepool.

"Brian is a true class act."

Bryan Robson, Manager of Middlesbrough:
"Players like Brian deserve everything they get in their testimonial year. People get carried away with the wages Premier League players get and think it is the same in lower leagues. These players need testimonial years to help towards things like their mortgage, when their career ends.

"A lot of people knock testimonials but it easy for players to move on and try and make a bit of money in their career, so when a player is loyal to a club he deserves this."

Alan Murray, former Hartlepool United Manager:
"As the country gets ready to say hello to another football season, we are gathered here to say goodbye to a very special player. Brian Honour has no England caps, no Cup Winners medals and no place in the Football Hall of Fame.

"But to many people, myself included, he will always be a player to remember. In my time in football I have come across all sorts of players, skilful, hard, dedicated, professional, determined, honest, likeable and popular. In Brian Honour I had the lot - in one player.

"He won't thank me for embarrassing him by saying it, but it was a pleasure working with Brian. He was never a spot of bother and when he pulled on the blue and white I knew he would give 100% for 90 minutes EVERY time."

Gary Henderson, Physio, Hartlepool United:
"I have worked with Brian for the last eight years. In that time I am proud to say we have become good friends. Everyone knows that Brian had more than his fair share of injuries and operations. Few know of the dedication and sheer hard work required to overcome those injuries not once, but time and time again. Brian has recently been christened Mr HUFC, and

surely no one deserves it more. His popularity says everything about him. One of the biggest compliments I can pay Brian is that of all the people I have met in and out of football not one person has had a bad word to say about him."

Harold Hornsey, Chairman, Hartlepool United:
"Brian Honour has been a great asset to Hartlepool United over the period of ten years he has been with us. He has been an excellent professional and a credit to the club in particular and to football in general. His commitment to Hartlepool has been a shining example to young players. He has had a great testimonial year."

Joe Allon, former Hartlepool striker and later Chelsea:
"What can you say about 'Wor Jackie'? Down to earth as they come, a very strong family man who dotes on his wife Janet and his two beautiful daughters. I had the pleasure of his company both on and off the park for two and a half years and maintain that he was the cog that started our promotion engine turning. He could have easily played at a higher level but for the fact of uprooting his family. A testimonial is fitting for this bloke who deserves it for his magnificent service and loyalty. Loved by the players, adored by the fans, for this Geordie boy, Brian Honour, is the heart in Hartlepool."

Billy Horner, former Manager Hartlepool United:
"What can be said about Brian Honour that has not already been said about him? I first saw Brian at Tow Law, playing for Peterlee on a cold winter night, show some good touch and some outstanding enthusiasm, which he still shows in everything he does.

"He is the type of player managers come to rely on, with his consistent displays throughout the season. It is really amazing that a bigger club never snapped him up because Brian could have certainly played at a higher level.

"Not only has Brian always been a good professional footballer, he has always been a pleasure to work with and when he comes into the dressing room with his bubbly personality and sense of humour, he can brighten anyone up."

Dave Latimer, Chairman, HUFC Supporters Association:
"Brian Honour is the player all the fans would be if we were to go out on the pitch in a Pools shirt. I have watched the club for 30 years and, in terms of total commitment and skill, I would rate him the number one player. No one has a bad word to say about Brian and you can see why, the way he puts his heart and soul into every minute. Normally at Pools we get players who are just here for a couple of years before moving on, but in Brian we have had a player who has given great service for his whole career.

"Congratulations, Mr Nice guy!"

Neil Watson, former Sports Editor, *Hartlepool Mail*:
"Reporting on Hartlepool United is a job many fans would relish. Just imagine, watching League football week in and week out, the occasional big cup game, mixing with the players. And getting paid for it too!

"But it is not always easy. I reported on Hartlepool's progress before the promotion season, when attention focused more often on the bottom half of the Fourth Division than the top. It is part of the reporter's job to voice an opinion on the team, and to be critical where necessary.

"I had my run ins.

"Manager John Bird more than once had a few harsh words when he felt I had gone too far. He even brought to an end a long tradition of the *Mail* reporter travelling with the team to away games.

"However, I have a lot of respect for John and feel he did a very good job at Hartlepool. He was desperate for success and gave everything to the cause. His criticisms of me were always in private, unlike my criticisms of Pool which were rather more public.

"Roy Hogan once felt I had gone too far in my criticisms of him during what I saw as a particularly poor spell of form. And

Dean Gibb objected when I described him as a 'headless chicken'. Aidan McCaffery and Alan Kennedy both left the club after my criticism of their displays in Hartlepool shirts, though that was probably more as a result of the manager having a similar opinion of their performances than the power of the *Mail*.

"The Sports Editor of the *Mail*, Roy Kelly, occasionally reminds me of a comment I once made in the paper.

"It read; 'Honour then slipped into the mediocrity that his teammates were still trying to achieve.'

"That is not the most flattering comment that will feature Brian in this souvenir, but it does show that more often than not Brian was leading the way for his teammates.

"I cannot remember ever criticising Brian. The only possible reason I can think of would be an occasional tendency to be over-physical, though even that was probably not as often as fans remember. Even then, it was not vicious. Brian just sometimes got carried away in the Hartlepool cause.

"I am sure everyone else paying tribute to Brian will say the same: you could not meet a nicer bloke.

"When he was forced to quit through injury, the *Mail* gave the story a big show.

"The recently appointed editor of the paper, Chris Cox, was a bit sceptical of the awe in which Brian was held. Then he met Brian at a testimonial dinner and became a convert. It was as a result of that meeting that Brian became a regular columnist in the *Mail Sports Special*.

"It was our small way of recognising his influence at the club over his ten years there and his character came through in his writing.

"He was always keen to see the positive side of the game and to pass on enthusiasm and experience to youngsters at the club.

"That is why I believe his appointment as part of the coaching team at the club is a major boost and thoroughly deserved. People like Brian Honour do not come along very often, and you have to keep them when they do."

The Hartlepool United Testimonial Team:

The Defence

The goalkeepers for Hartlepool that day were Kevin Poole and Brian Cox. Kevin had just completed a year with Premiership Leicester City and was brought in for the final run-in to promotion in 1990-91 by Alan Murray. Brian Cox laid the foundations during the season.

The Hartlepool defence turning out for Brian comprised Keith Nobbs, Rob McKinnon, Mick Smith, John MacPhail and Ian Bennyworth.

Keith Nobbs was almost as popular as Brian. He holds the record for clearing the ball into the street more than any other defender. He and the goalkeeper provided the headline writers with many potentially illegal opportunities. Nobbs has remained with Hartlepool United since he retired and is very much involved in Football in the Community.

Mick Smith was another popular player whose career was cruelly ended by injury. Opposition beware - he is now a bobby.

John McPhail was dominant centre half whose power and experience proved so vital in Pool's promotion glory. Born in Dundee, John played for Sheffield United, York City (where twice he was the Player of the Season), Bristol City and Sunderland as well as 163 times for Hartlepool United, in a career total of more than 600 games in which he scored 58 goals.

Ian Bennyworth made his mark as a defender during the promotion campaign after being signed by the late great Cyril Knowles. Ian played at Scarborough when another Pools legend Neil Warnock was there. Warnock became a Premier League manager.

Rob McKinnon, everybody said, was too good for the Third and Fourth Divisions and he's proved it since. An honorary Hartlepudlian, he is now a Scottish international and nobody deserves that honour more. Rob was a model professional at Hartlepool United and performed with distinction many times in the blue and white of Pools. His three international caps were little reward for a career spanning two millennia and with more than 500 appearances both at home and abroad.

The Midfield

The midfield comprised Don Hutchinson, Paul Olsson, John Tinkler and Andy Davies.

John Tinkler was a midfield player from Trimdon who, like Brian, always enjoyed playing for his local league club. John played over 200 games for Hartlepool as well as playing for Preston North End and Walsall.

Paul Olsson now plays for another club somewhere in County Durham, but just for now we will forgive him for that. He scored some great goals from midfield. Paul played for Hull City, Exeter City and Scarborough as well as the 'old enemy' Darlington.

Don Hutchinson was another player who made good after leaving the Vic. Following his success at Liverpool he is now at West Ham where his skills are appreciated by the London fans. Don played for Liverpool, West Ham, Everton, Sheffield United, Sunderland, Millwall, Coventry and Scotland, being awarded 26 international caps and commanding transfer fees totalling in excess of £10 million in various moves.

Andy Davies settled at Hartlepool after Cyril signed him from Torquay United - another adopted Hartlepudlian. He played in the promotion team before returning to Torquay.

The Forwards

The forwards included Ricardo Gabbiadini, Joe Allon, Paul Dalton, Anthony Skedd, Paul Baker and, of course, Brian himself.

Ricardo Gabbiadini wasn't with Hartlepool long, but he made an impression and it was good to have him back for the testimonial. Ricardo played just 19 games for Pools, scoring three goals. His clubs included York, Sunderland, Scarborough and Carlisle, although he was loaned out on several occasions to Blackpool, Grimsby Town, Brighton and

Hove Albion and Crewe.

Geordie striker Joe Allon is the only player from one of the smaller clubs to have been named North East Player of the Year. Another ex-Magpie, Joe became a folk hero for his goals and rapport with the crowd. Joe joined Pools from Swansea City in 1988 and, after a slow start, he top-scored with 17 goals in 1989-90, followed by a club record of 35 when Pools won promotion in 1990-91. Allon left for Chelsea in the summer of 1991 but failed to win a regular place at Stamford Bridge. After a series of moves he rejoined Pools in 1995 and finished as top scorer twice more before retiring through injury. Joe now works for Leeds United.

Paul Dalton is yet another success story. He was a spectacular winger and his new club, Plymouth, deserved to be more successful than it has been since he went there. Paul's career was spent at Brandon United, Manchester United and Pools, where in 177 appearances he scored 43 goals and was an important member of the promotion side. After leaving Pools he also played for Huddersfield Town, Carlisle United, Gateshead, Dunston Federation and Billingham Town.

Anthony Skedd, the youngest member of the squad, was included because he had never made any secret of the fact that Brian Honour was his hero. We know how you feel, Skeddy.

Paul Baker was one of the club's greatest ever forwards, scoring 14 times in his first 11 games for Pools, before joining Gillingham. However, he is nearer home again now. Did you know he is Lee Clark's brother-in-law? During his playing career he graced the fields of Bishop Auckland, Southampton, Carlisle United, Motherwell, Gillingham, York City, Torquay United, Scunthorpe and Arbroath, and was a manager at Hartlepool, Blyth Spartans and Newcastle Benfield.

Finally in the forward line was a little fella called Brian Honour, of course, and there has never been a more popular Hartlepool United player. The fact that Kevin Keegan and Newcastle agreed to the testimonial game shows that his career had not gone unnoticed.

The team was managed by Alan Murray.

The men in black were Ian Cruikshanks, the referee, Ken Powell and Dave Lowes, the linesmen, and the fourth official was M. Readman.

Newcastle United:

The Defence

The goalkeepers were Mike Hooper and Pavel Srnicek and the rest of the defence team comprised Warren Barton, Marc Hottiger, Steve Watson, John Beresford, Steve Howey, Philippe Albert and Darren Peacock.

The Czech keeper has emerged as a fans' favourite since his move from Banik Ostrava, holding off the challenge of Mike Hooper for the goalkeeper's jersey. Pavel Srnicek was only released by Sam Allerdyce in 2007. In the interim period he played for West Ham and Sheffield Wednesday as well as the Magpies and he collected 49 international caps along the way.

Mike Hooper, formerly with Liverpool, was a formidable opponent and a superb deputy for Kevin Keegan to call upon when needed. Mike played for Bristol City and Wrexham and also at Liverpool where he acted as understudy to Bruce Grobbelaar. He moved to Newcastle via Leicester and is one of the many players to hold a graduate degree. Mike's is in English Literature, so no doubt he will have his thoughts on this publication. Last heard he was working in Durham City.

Warren Barton signed in the closed season from Wimbledon for £4 million. Barton was expected to press his England claims with the Magpies and had already forced his way into the reckoning, making his debut in the ill-fated friendly with Ireland in Dublin earlier that year.

Marc Hottiger was a Swiss fullback who signed for Newcastle after an impressive World Cup campaign in America. He played in his homeland for Lausanne Sport 168 times and for FC Sion 149 times, but he also graced the fields of Goodison Park as well as Newcastle. He played for Switzerland 63 times, scoring five goals.

Steve Watson was only 21 years of age and was a local lad

made good. He was yet to establish himself as a first team regular, but he had made plenty of appearances in a variety of positions. He played 208 times for Newcastle in every position. He was transferred to Villa and then on to Everton, where he made 125 starts. He then moved to West Brom and looks like finishing his career at Sheffield Wednesday, where he signed a two-year contract in 2007. He achieved one England 'B' cap in 1998.

John Beresford joined Newcastle from Portsmouth and has proved a very consistent performer ever since. An attacking fullback, he likes to join the attack whenever possible. John played at Barnsley and Portsmouth before joining Newcastle, where he made 179 appearances and scored three goals. He later went to Southampton and Birmingham City and clocked up a career total of more than 400 games, including two caps as an England 'B' international.

Steve Howey was just 23 years of age. He has established himself in the full England squad and will be looking for a good year in the Premiership as the European Championships loom just around the corner. Steve eventually made 191 appearances in the black and white before moving to Manchester City, Leicester City and Bolton, and for one game, in 2005, he played for Hartlepool United. He had spells at Boro as a youth coach and for a time worked with Brian Honour as his assistant at Bishop Auckland. This versatile young man achieved four full England caps.

Philippe Albert, the controversial Belgian World Cup star, is sadly missing from the field after suffering a horrible long-term injury. Fans will be hoping he makes a full recovery and a quick return to the Magpies line-up. Philippe became a cult figure at St James and his most famous moment, which is played time and time again, was his audacious chip over Peter Schmeichel in the famous 5-0 win over Manchester United. Winner of the Belgian Golden Shoe award, Philippe played for Newcastle 96 times before moving on to Fulham, and he achieved 42 international caps for Belgium. He is now retired and working as a pundit for Belgian TV.

Darren Peacock was a highly rated former QPR defender, who has teamed up again with former Loftus Road teammate Les Ferdinand. Kevin Keegan brought Darren to St James Park for £2.4 million. He had played for Newport, Hereford United and QPR before joining Newcastle, and then had spells for Blackburn Rovers and Wolves. He is now thought to be living in Portugal with his family.

Midfield

The midfield players comprised Scott Sellers, Lee Clark, Robert Lee, David Ginola and Peter Beardsley.

Scott Sellers, a silk midfielder with a sweet left foot, is another player who suffered from injury last season and whose absence made a marked impression on the side. Scott is truly the £700k man. He was bought from Leeds United for £700k and sold for £700k to Bolton Wanderers.

Lee Clark, only 22 years old, was a running midfielder with black and white blood running through his veins. He played more than 200 games for Newcastle United in two spells, with excursions to near neighbours Sunderland and Fulham. He became involved in management and last heard was at Delia Smith's Norwich City. "Come on let's be 'aving you."

Robert Lee signed from Charlton. His golden start in midfield with Newcastle United soon earned him England recognition. He was born in West Ham but signed for Charlton Athletic, where he made almost 300 appearances, scoring 59 goals. His move to Newcastle saw him turn out in the Magpie colours 303 times and score 44 goals before moving to Derby County, West Ham and Wycombe Wanderers in a career that boasted more than 700 appearances, 105 goals and 21 England caps and, in the three lions shirt, two goals.

David Ginola was United's new French superstar and could bring the same Gallic flair to Newcastle that Eric Cantona does to Manchester United. David was unkindly referred to as 'The Frog on the Tyne', an obvious reference to the popular hit song. Before he arrived on Tyneside he made 308 appearances in his native France. He played for Newcastle 58 times, scoring six goals, before going south to Tottenham Hotspur, where 100 appearances reaped 13 goals and the 1999 PFA Player of the Year award. He did time at Villa and Everton and along the way picked up 17 caps for France, scoring three goals.

Peter Beardsley - inspirational - 'nuf said! Peter played initially for Carlisle 104 times before going to Canada to play for Vancouver 81 times, scoring 30 goals. During his first spell at Newcastle he had 147 starts, producing an incredible 61 goals, and he was signed by Liverpool. He played more than 200 games on Merseyside, 131 for the red half of the city and 81 for Everton, scoring more than 70 goals before coming home to Newcastle United. He made a further 129 appearances, scoring 46 goals, before going to Bolton, Manchester City and Fulham as well as playing 22 glorious games at Hartlepool United. Peter Beardsley was once described by Gary Lineker as the best strike partner he had ever had, and he picked up 59 England international caps.

Forwards

The forwards comprised Les Ferdinand, Keith Gillespie, Paul Kitson and Ruel Fox, and the Newcastle United manager was Kevin Keegan.

Les Ferdinand had a lot to live up to but had what it takes to become another centre forward legend with Newcastle. He was great in the air, with pace and power to boot. 'Sir Les', as he is affectionately known in the game, came to Newcastle for £6 million from QPR, where he scored 80 goals in just 163 games. After his stay in the north he went to Spurs for £6 million before playing at West Ham, Leicester, Bolton and Reading. He scored five goals for England in just 17 games and, although not knighted by Her Majesty the Queen, was given an MBE in 2005.

Keith Gillespie, the Northern Ireland international, was cast in the role of makeweight in the deal that sent Andy Cole to Old Trafford, but he soon showed what a valuable acquisition he was. Keith played 78 times in the green of Northern Ireland

and 113 times in the black and white of Newcastle. He also played for Manchester United, Wigan, Blackburn Rovers, Leicester City and Sheffield United. On his day he could travel.

Paul Kitson was a big money buy from Derby, but struggled to fill Andy Cole's boots. Paul was born in Murton, County Durham. He played for Leicester City, Derby County, West Ham United, Charlton Athletic, Crystal Palace, Brighton, Rushden & Diamonds, Aldershot Town and Newcastle United. He signed for West Ham for £2.3 million, making his debut against Spurs in 1997 and scoring. Paul is now thought to be living at Wynyard on Teesside.

Winger Ruel Fox signed from Norwich City. He played just 58 games for Newcastle, scoring 12 goals. He is best remembered by fans at Norwich City, where 173 games produced 22 goals and he was inducted into the Canaries Hall of Fame. He also played for Spurs and West Brom, and as well as one 'B' international cap with England he went on to gain two full international caps with Montserrat and score a goal before becoming national coach.

This is the calibre of the players that turned out to honour Brian.

A Word from Kevin Keegan OBE:

"It was Lee Clark who first asked me if we could help Brian Honour and I was delighted to be able to say that we could. It is entirely fitting that a lifelong Newcastle United supporter should have his favourite club for his testimonial game, especially as it's the match in which we parade our new signings. It's fitting, too, that I should help a man who helped me - Brian was at St James Park when I made my debut against Queen's Park Rangers back in August 1982.

"Brian's love affair with Newcastle has never waned and I happen to know that his Father's Day present this year was one of our new Adidas shirts!

"The Brian Honours of football are really unsung heroes, the guys who give their level best every time they play, rarely making the headlines but thoroughly enjoy their playing careers. Brian's was cut short by injury, but long before that he had bounced back from the dole queue after serving his apprenticeship with Darlington.

"He doesn't need me to tell him that there's a lot of money kicking around in the game these days. He also doesn't need me to remind him that he hasn't made a great deal out of football.

"But you can't put a price on respect from your fellow professionals and fans, and in that sense Brian Honour not only enriched the game he loves with a passion, but also ended his professional playing days worth a good deal more than many of his contemporaries.

"My only regret is that the Victoria Ground does not hold 50,000.

"What's for sure is that every penny he makes from the match, we're so pleased to be taking part in, is richly deserved. This man has been an absolute credit to his profession."

Janet Honour, Brian's wife, wrote as her contribution to the testimonial day:

"When I first started courting Brian he was already a young professional at Darlington. However, I had known him many years before this as we lived in the same street as youngsters. He was the little lad kicking a ball against the wall at the bottom of the street. He would always take pleasure in trying to hit me with the ball as I walked by!

"Being the wife of a professional footballer has its good points and bad points. I have learned to live with his many moods.

"He was always unhappy when he was out injured or was playing badly or if the team had been beaten. Brian hates being beaten.

"Good points include long holidays in the summer, with plenty of time to spend together with me and our two daughters, Sarah and Laura.

"But during the season he spent a lot of time away from

home, travelling up and down the country.

"This was the case when I was expecting our first child in March 1988.

"Pools were playing away at Torquay and Exeter and were staying all week.

"The inevitable happened. I was taken into hospital to have the baby.

"Brian kept in touch every hour or so by telephone, but it was still a shame for him having to miss out on the birth of our first daughter.

"He loved playing for Pools so much that it is hard to think of him doing something else. But that time has come.

"But whatever develops in his career, Brian can be sure of full support from me and the girls."

When I met Janet in the winter of 2007, she was 'still standing by her man'. The family have moved from their old terraced house in Blackhall Colliery to a modern detached 'at the top of the hill'.

You just know that that is where Brian and Janet should be.

Samantha Lee looked at Brian's five favourite goals in the programme entitled 'Five Star Honour'. Samantha now runs her own company in Hartlepool - Publicity Seekers - and is treasurer of the North East Football Writers Association.

Brian may not be remembered for a tremendous goalscoring record, but when the little man hit the back of the net it was more often than not in spectacular fashion. The midfielder managed a total of 29 goals in his ten years at Pool, but five in particular stand out for the hero of the Vic. In time-honoured fashion, Sam Lee put the goals in reverse order:

* Goal No. 5: Hartlepool United 1, Crystal Palace 1; 25th September 1991, Rumbelows Cup, second round, first leg.

* Goal No. 4: Hartlepool United 3, Southend United 2; 12th April 1986; Football League Division Four.

* Goal No. 3: Maidstone 1, Hartlepool United 4; 23rd March 1991.

* Goal No. 2: Hartlepool United 2, Stockport County 1; 24th August 1993; Coca Cola Cup, first round, second leg.

* Goal No. 1: Sunderland 0, Hartlepool United 1; 9th February 1988; Freight Rover Trophy.

If you were to ask Brian Honour to name the man who played the biggest role in his career, his reply would not be that of a player or manager. The man in question would be physiotherapist Gary Henderson, whose healing hands pushed Brian's playing days on at times when injury seem certain to end them.

A knee injury sustained at Orient in the spring of 1988 put the midfielder on the sidelines and forced him to spend two punishing summers in a painful bid to regain his fitness.

Brian says, "If it had not been for Gary, I probably wouldn't have come back. He saved my career. Gary was an absolute godsend. For two summers he took a lot of his spare time to help me. I can't thank him enough."

These are some of the press reports at the time:

Roy Kelly, Sports Editor, *Hartlepool Mail*:
"NOT being the world's greatest footballer myself, I found my way into sport by writing about it.

"Having watched Pool from being a kid, I remember Brian's first season at the club and every subsequent one and I would have given my right arm to have played on the same team as him.

"I never dreamt that I would ever be in the same side as Brian. But last season he was to join our 'team' at the Mail Sports Special after his footballing career was ended by injury, writing the 'Life of Brian' column.

"Just as he was a tremendous footballer, Brian became an excellent columnist, writing from the heart with great honesty and conviction.

"I had to echo the words many a footballer and manager have said, that Brian is a pleasure to work with. Brian is a true professional and a true gentleman.

"Brian continued to take an interest in writing long after his journalist career with the Mail ended. You are reading his latest contribution as he says, "assisted by my 'new' friend and 'old' Hartlepool United stalwart John Riddle", now the sports editor of a newspaper in the Canary Islands."

Simon Turnbull, Chief Sports Writer, *Northern Echo*:

"If I had to pick a North East Xl from five seasons on the region's beat for the *Northern Echo* it would be a toss-up whether the first name on the sheet would be Peter Beardsley or Brian Honour.

"Beardsley's second spell as a Newcastle player has been a joy to behold. In terms of vision, craft and guile, he has to rank alongside Kenny Dalglish as the best of British in the past two decades.

"Brian Honour, as a foot soldier of the Toon Army, whose players marvel at Beardsley's brilliance, would be the first to admit that the skills he showed in his ten years at Hartlepool United were not in the same class.

"But those who describe him as essentially a brave midfield battler would be doing him a great injustice.

"Brian Honour played with vision and a delicate touch at times, as well as with his customary whole-heartedness. He was the type of rock-solid inspirational player every team needs."

Sean Atkins, Sports Writer, *Hartlepool Mail*:

"Followers of Hartlepool United can look back on years of enjoyment provided by Brian Honour on the football pitch - I saw little more than a couple of hours from the man.

"But after a year covering Pool, it is clear to an outsider like myself that he has been the single most influential player here during the last decade or so. And that's not just because he had been there for a decade.

"Joe Allon might have scored more goals, Bob Newton might have been a more colourful character and Don

Hutchinson might have gone on to far greater things.

"But there is something about Honour that demands respect, compels you to like him.

"Hartlepool United and their fans have been lucky enough to have seen him and I was fortunate to have caught a glimpse."

The author of 'Life of Brian', John Riddle, echoes those comments from Sean:

"I saw most of Brian Honour's games but did not meet him until 2007. It's fair to say we met as strangers and after hours of interviews I am privileged to call him and his wife Janet - 'friends'."

Harry Blackwood, Deputy Editor, Hartlepool Mail:

"Salt of the earth, canny lad, smashing fella.

"Not the sort of terms of endearment one normally associates with professional footballers. But any of those descriptions, indeed all of them, are ideal to describe Hartlepool United's favourite son, Brian Honour.

"In his years at the Vic, Brian Honour turned the old-fashioned virtues of determination, hard work and integrity to his advantage to become a firm favourite with the fans. A fair helping of talent and a heart as big as a lion also came in handy.

"I remember Brian as one of the nicest lads I met during my travels with Hartlepool United during the short time I covered the club for the *Hartlepool Mail*. There were other nice lads, of course, but Brian always stood out as being genuine and unassuming.

"Helping others was never too much trouble. Whether it was minutes after coming off the pitch after a last-minute sickener or during a celebratory bag of fish and chips after a good win, the gentlemen of the press were always assured of a friendly smile and a modest quote from Brian.

"Out of millions of kids who dream of a career in professional football there are only a few who make it. Many of them soon forget their roots and allow fame and fortune to go to their heads.

"But you couldn't begrudge Brian anything he achieved in the game. If life was fair, and well no it isn't, fame and fortune would have been heaped on him in large doses on the certain knowledge that he would have been eternally grateful for it.

"Thousands of Pool fans have watched an ordinary working-class lad from the collieries give blood, sweat and tears for the club.

"He really is Hartlepool United's favourite son."

Arthur Pickering, TFM Reporter, Tyne Tees TV:
"In a quarter of a century of watching Hartlepool United as a journalist, I have seen a real assortment of players turn out for the club.

"Conmen, stars of the future, cheats, honest plodders, has-beens, liars, no-hopers, cowards, you name them they have all played for Pool.

"Not one player has ever been able to match Brian Honour in qualities he has brought to the Vic for the last decade: honesty, dedication, skill effort, professionalism. And he's scored a few memorable goals as well.

"I got to know him through his brother John, who used to play for Pool of course, and you can see some of him in Brian. Except that Brian can't sing.

"On the pitch, he's a character who always gives 100 per cent. Off it, he is like so many people from his part of the world - a canny lad.

"If you could get a team of 11 Brian Honours, you would never be outplayed, never humiliated, and never taken lightly. You might not win them all but you would have a hell of a crack at them, and be great entertainers as well.

"Of course, it's traditional for the likes of me to trot out the old 'what a good bloke' rubbish about players when they have testimonials.

"The difference here is that I mean it. Brian deserves every penny he gets because he is a good lad.

"Pity about that haircut!"

John Riddle, The Sports Editor of *The Paper* (an English language publication printed in Tenerife) writes:

"It is now more than 12 years since Brian Honour played his last game for Hartlepool United, apart from the odd appearance in the Masters. It is 12 years since his much publicised and praised testimonial against Kevin Keegan's Newcastle United.

"In the ensuing period what has happened to some of the teams that Brian faced in his eleven years at Hartlepool?

"Torquay United finished bottom of the League for three consecutive seasons in 1984-87 and are currently plying their trade in the Blue Square Premier League (the old Vauxhall Conference) and could be back in the League.

"Wolverhampton Wanderers ten years ago finished 4th in the Fourth Division and today they are in the Championship looking to go back into the top flight.

"The reason why I am stating these obvious facts is to show that because of the investment made by OIR and the chairman Ken Hodcroft in the next ten years it is possible to go up as well as down the football pyramid.

"In the Fourth Division on 7th May 1988 Bolton Wanderers finished in third spot behind Wolves and today they are playing in the Premiership. A 1-0 win at home to Manchester United took them clear of the relegation places and if Bolton can reach the dizzy heights of the Premiership in what is effectively one generation then could Hartlepool?

"On 2nd May 1992 just 15 years ago Brentford were promoted as champions and in second place Birmingham City. Languishing in the lower places at 9th were Fulham, Reading were in 12th, Wigan in 15th. All three clubs would rise through the divisions in the next decade or so to grace the Premiership.

"At the time of writing in the winter of 2007 Fulham, Birmingham, Reading and Wigan, all in Division Three in May 1992, are now in the top flight.

"In 1994 Reading were promoted as champions and we now know where they were headed.

"Sadly Pools were relegated along with Fulham and Barnet.

"Fulham recovered to get into the Premiership within a decade.

"Of course for every success story there are those who didn't quite make it.

"Halifax Town, Exeter City, Oxford United, York City, Cambridge United have all lost their League status and languish in the old Vauxhall Conference now renamed the Blue Square Premier League.

"Others have suffered an even worse fate!

"Scarborough Football Club appears to have died following going into liquidation, Newport County are playing in the old Conference South, and Rushden & Diamonds who pipped us on the final day of the season in the race for the Championship are now also in the old Vauxhall Conference.

"Fortunes can change in football as Brian Honour knows and his career was certainly a ride on the 'Big Dipper' of life he is likely never to forget."

Drunk at Darlington - Allegedly!

Many stories have been told about a Hartlepool United game at Darlington on 29 September 1997 and an incident involving Brian Honour. At the time, Brian was at the match as a spectator and not in any capacity with the football club.

He had joined his pals at the Mill House public house in Hartlepool, before they all made their way through to Darlington. Brian readily admits to having one or two drinks in the Mill House - well that's what customers do in pubs.

Brian takes up the story:

"Mickey Brown scored for Pools (he was on loan for six games from Manchester City) and there was a big stand-off and a clash with rival fans.

"I saw a friend of mine behaving in an irresponsible manner, climbing on the makeshift chicken-wire type fence. I could see he would get himself into trouble. I approached the fence, pulled him away and told him to calm down. I thought no more about the incident.

"Janet and I went on holiday to Benidorm in the June. When we returned from our time in the sun, neighbours advised us that the police had been to the house. They had apparently come to the house at 5 a.m. and cordoned off the street. I wondered why they wanted me."

A few weeks later Brian's daughter Sarah, aged 9, was knocked over in a serious car accident, breaking her arm and legs. She was hospitalised and his wife Janet spent each night in hospital with her while Brian stayed at home and looked after the younger child.

One night while Janet was at the hospital Brian retired for the night, making sure that the youngest child, aged 8, was asleep. Then at 5 a.m. he was awoken by a knock at the door.

Slipping on his dressing gown, he went to the door to be confronted by two burly police officers.

"Are you Brian Honour?" one asked.

"Yes, that's me," replied Brian, thinking there was a problem with the child in hospital.

"Brian Honour, we are arresting you on a charge of football violence," said one officer.

Brian invited the police inside, where they undertook a search of the house - looking for what, Brian has no idea. He never saw a search warrant but wasn't too worried because he had nothing to hide.

"You will have to come with us to Darlington Police Station," explained one copper.

Brian protested his innocence and added that he couldn't go with them as his youngest daughter was asleep upstairs and his wife and other child were in hospital. His protests were in vein and the police 'invited' him to get the child out of bed and dressed and then take her round to a neighbour.

It was raining and dark and the police action appeared a little heavy-handed. But Brian complied with their 'request' and the bemused and frightened child was placed with a neighbour.

Brian was taken to Darlington Police Station, charged and then bailed and allowed to return home - so what really was the purpose of arresting him and taking him away at the crack of dawn?

Brian at the time declined legal representation. He had done nothing wrong. He was shown a video of the incident and still could not see why he was being charged.

The problem, which Brian still maintains today, was due to poor segregation and an inadequate fence at the ageing Feethams ground.

In the next year Brian Honour attended Darlington Magistrates Court on more than four occasions. He became quite friendly with the Quaker fans who had also been charged and the Hartlepool travelling support caught up in the melee.

Brian maintained his innocence throughout, reiterating his account that he was merely trying to prevent trouble.

When the matter was committed to Teesside Crown Court, Brian decided he should engage the services of a solicitor. So he went to see Mr John Elwood of the Hartlepool firm Tilley, Bailey and Irvine. It was a wise move and Brian received plenty of expert advice and support from the solicitor.

For a full 12 months this court case hung over Brian like a black cloud. What people didn't know as fact, they simply added to the story anyway. Many had the little man found guilty even before the trial.

Brian was told to present himself at Teesside Crown Court and be prepared for a trial that could last two to three weeks.

On the Monday the various defendants were called to discussions with their barristers. By lunchtime Brian was still waiting to see his brief.

The Darlington fans were offered a deal to the effect that if they pleaded guilty to a lesser charge the judge was prepared to give them shorter jail sentences of three months. Of course such deals are never proffered in British courts, but this is what the lads were told and so they accepted the offer. One of these Hartlepool lads was 'Big Kev' aka 'Shamrock', who used to stand in the north-east corner of the Mill House stand.

Kev and Brian and the Darlington lads went to lunch together. During lunch Kev rang his mother and advised her that he may not be coming home at the end of the day.

Brian did not enjoy his lunch because he had been offered nothing. He was naturally worried even though he still maintained he had done nothing wrong.

When he returned to court he was told by his solicitor, Mr Elwood, that the Judge Peter Fox had reviewed the evidence, including the video footage, and would be instructing the jury to discharge the matter. The other people involved in the alleged incident, including 'Big Kev', received a fine rather than a custodial sentence.

The alleged incident had a profound effect on Brian Honour and his family that year. His injured daughter was eventually released from hospital and returned home. The family were reunited. The nightmare was over.

Moving into Management at Hartlepool United

Brian Honour was in charge of Hartlepool United for just seven games before Chris Turner arrived in 1999.

Tommy Miller scored twice in Brian's first game in charge in round two of the Associate Members Cup, when they drew 2-2 with Preston North End at the Vic. However, four days later, on a trip to Humberside, the Hartlepool team failed to score and Hull City ran out winners 4-0. Then on 26th January, in round three of the Associate Members Cup, Pools lost at home to Lincoln City with only 1,370 fans turning up to watch the game.

Brian's first win as boss was achieved at Spotland when Clarke scored to give Pools a 1-0 win at Rochdale. Then back home a week later Brian doubled his success when Howard scored twice in the 2-0 win over Halifax Town.

More than 3,900 turned up for the game against Brian's former club Darlington on 13th February. Tommy Miller scored again, supported by Irvine, but the 13th was unlucky for Brian as Pools lost 3-2.

An away defeat at Exeter City on 20th February brought to an end Brian's seven-match reign as manager of Hartlepool United.

Pools were in 22nd position in the League when Brian handed over to Chris Turner, and they finished the season in exactly the same position, 3rd from bottom, with Scarborough losing their League status. Hartlepool avoided the drop by just four points.

Tommy Miller was one of the most successful products of the Hartlepool Youth Academy system. Tommy made his first team debut in October 1997. Two years later his contribution made him a regular in the Pools team and Brian Honour selected Tommy to play in his team. Miller finished as top scorer in 1990-2000 and 2000-01 and was included in the Professional Footballers Association Team of the Year on both occasions.

Tommy signed for Ipswich Town, then in the Premier League, in the summer of 2001 for a record fee of £750,000. Tommy has been kind enough to share some of his memories of his footballing years and of Brian Honour:

"As a young boy growing up, my dad used to take me to plenty of football matches across the north-east. Hartlepool was the closest having been brought up in Shotton Colliery.

"I was fortunate to be the mascot when Hartlepool United played Luton Town in 1988 in the FA Cup Round 3.

"My favourite two players at the time were Paul Baker and Brian Honour. Although they lost the game that day, it was a wonderful experience meeting the players and running out at the Vic having just turned nine years old. My photograph appeared in the programme too.

"Many years passed and having been released by Ipswich Town as a schoolboy just before I turned 16 years old I thought my dream of becoming a professional footballer had ended.

"That was until I came across a certain Brian Honour once again.

"My dad was manager of Shotton Boys. He had known Brian for quite a few years and asked him if he could come and do a bit of coaching for his team at the Peterlee Leisure Centre. I went along to join in a few times and Brian, who was working with the Hartlepool youth team at the time, asked me to come down and train with the other YTS players at the football club. The rest, as they say, is history. I went down to train and after about a week Billy Horner offered me a two-year YTS scheme, which I obviously accepted.

"My dream of becoming a professional footballer was back on.

"After my two-year YTS scheme I was offered a professional contract. I made my Football League debut not long after against Chester City. I went on to play around 140 games before leaving for Ipswich Town in 2001.

"Since them days I have remained very good friends with Brian and his lovely wife Janet and speak to him regularly.

"Brian Honour is a very good coach and hopefully he will be back in full-time football as a manager or coach. He has a lot to offer and the game needs characters like Brian."

Durham City

Brian Honour would then move on to manage Durham City. He was reasonably successful and at one stage had a run of six straight wins, which came to a halt in November 2000 with a defeat at Morpeth. Brian acknowledged that all good things come to an end soon, but a lot of players had an off day.

In February 2001 Brian welcomed to Durham City new signing Richard Ord. The former Sunderland player was forced to quit the professional game after being injured playing at QPR and Brian persuaded Richard to join him at Durham City. Ord made his debut in the 2-1 win at West Auckland and Honour said, "He was a different class, organising the team and talking to the younger lads." Brian realised that getting Ord to Durham would stabilise the team and be a real asset to them.

However, injuries badly affected the City side, and before the game with Dunston, Brian Honour was without ten first-team players.

In November 2001 Brian was still at City but was struggling with his rebuilding of the Durham team, who were 8th in the table. In the Durham Challenge Cup Durham City were stunned by Second Division club Horden. Brian was beginning to lose patience with some of his players.

"Horden wanted to win the game more than us. That upset me. I had a long chat with the chairman and some of the Durham City players had gone as far as they could. I had doubts about some after we suffered a defeat at Bedlington Terriers and this result against Horden just confirmed it," Brian explained.

In February 2002 Brian was interviewed by a local paper and he shared that interview with me from his scrapbook.

Durham City, known as 'The Citizens', were to play one of

their biggest games since they were ejected from the old Third Division (North) almost 75 years earlier.

City were one of three Northern League sides left in the last 16 of the FA Vase and had a home tie with St Neots. City had former Sunderland players Richard Ord and Gary Bennett, the latter being part of the management structure at Darlington until a week before the game.

Brian, who had 20 years as a pro, commented that with Ord and Bennett and the other lads there was a buzz about the City.

Richard Ord joined Sunderland as an Associate Schoolboy in 1984 and graduated through their academy to become a full-time pro in July 1987. Dickie, as he was known, made his League debut for the Black Cats in November 1987. That was in Sunderland's best win for 30 years when they thrashed Southend 7-0. The fans loved him as much as Pools fans adored Brian Honour and they often sang his praises with the ditty "Who needs Cantona when we've got Dickie Ord?" Praise indeed.

Dickie was transferred to Queens Park Rangers for £1 million, but it is for his time at Sunderland that he will be remembered. The last we heard he was running a pub, like so many ex-pros of his era, in Durham City.

Gary Bennett played alongside Richard Ord at Sunderland. Bennett was signed for £65,000 in July 1984 and played 389 times for Sunderland, scoring 23 goals. In the twilight of his career he also played at Carlisle and Scarborough and then finally at Darlington where he was also manager. He now works as a radio and TV pundit, commenting on games at Sunderland.

This was only 'Little Jackie's' apprenticeship in the managerial stakes, but he said he was loving every minute of it. The banter, the camaraderie and the rivalry of the Northern League were every bit as fierce as the Football League, where he spent so many years with Hartlepool United.

The Blackhall lad was still only 37 years old, unassuming, talkative and with a football brain as sharp as the wind off the west dock on the Marina. A reporter at the time quipped that

Brian could become a successful manager even with the team in Durham Prison. Then he could use the headline 'Honour among thieves'.

Some hacks will do anything for a cheap laugh!

The reporter then recounted Brian's days at Villa and Darlington, which I have already shared with you, from Peterlee during the miners' strike to his arrival at Hartlepool.

Brian said at the time, "I always tried to give 100% and I think the Hartlepool fans appreciated that."

They most certainly did and they enjoyed the banter he had with the lads in the Mill House stand. Stewart Dawson, the City chairman and the man with the vision behind the New Ferens Park, saw Brian one day coaching some youngsters. He takes up the story:

"I'd known Jackie for years and I didn't realise how good a coach he was. Even though those kids were coming off the field knackered, they had broad smiles on their faces ... because Brian made it interesting," he explained.

"The lads at the time probably didn't realise how much knowledge Brian passed on to them, but it was clear to the chairman that he had a rapport with everyone who came into contact with him.

"But after two months of this season Brian was ready to call it a day at City. They had lost to Horden in the League Cup from the Division below. This was a bitter blow to Brian, as all his family and friends from Blackhall, just up the road, had witnessed the defeat. Then Durham lost 3-1 at home to League champions Bedlington.

"Brian felt he had gone as far as he could with the team and that maybe a new man at the helm was needed."

But the senior players and the supportive chairman persuaded him to stay for the time being. But some of the players appeared to be well past their sell-by date. Oh, they were fit enough and they were great leaders on the field, but there does come a time when your legs do say 'I have had enough'.

Brian switched to a 4-4-2 formation, which brought the

wingers into play more often.

At this time, as at other times in his colourful career, Brian Honour lived, breathed, ate and drank football - for six days a week. But he reserved every Sunday for Mrs Honour and his beautiful daughters!

Bishop Auckland

In April 2004, now manager at Bishop Auckland, Brian appealed for the fans to turn out in force when they tried to clinch promotion against Farsley Celtic.

Bishops' 0-0 draw at 4th-placed Lincoln United the previous Saturday had put them in pole position for the last promotion place. Bishops were being pursued by five clubs, and they needed two points for 13th place and promotion.

Honour said: "The game against Celtic was probably to be the most important match Bishop Auckland played for a very long time.

"It would be a tough game, because Farsley beat us nine days previous, but I was confident the lads would be up for it. It was in our own hands.

"One thing we needed to make sure of was not having to go to Witton Albion on needing to win. I thought we picked up a good point the previous week, because Lincoln still had a chance of winning the League."

Bishops almost won the game, but Stuart Irvine hit the post from a free kick and Shaun Hope's header was well saved. Lincoln went close through Tony Simmons in the dying seconds.

In October 2005 Brian looked certain to quit Bishop Auckland as their manager. He had been in charge for three years and the Cup exit at the hands of Skelmersdale prompted him to tender his resignation. Brian explained that it had been a bit of a roller-coaster ride and tough as well considering all the circumstances. He felt a change for the club would be good - a new voice, as he put it.

Brian had used every ounce of his footballing knowledge, but found it impossible to replace the 15 players who had left the club. He had tried to strengthen the squad, but had lost out more than a few times to Northern League clubs.

"I knew the results had not been good enough and going down to Skelmersdale, well that hurt me a lot. We should have won considering the chances we had and if you don't put your chances away, well this is the result," Brian explained.

"I felt at the time I had given the manager's job at Bishop Auckland my all. I could do no more. Some people were linking me with the vacant job at Gateshead, but a job on the Tyne had nothing to do with my decision. It was the results.

"I had great backing from the players, the supporters, the owners, but I felt it was time to move on."

Tony Duffy, the vice chairman at Bishops responded, "Brian has worked hard. He has been very honest with us throughout his time here. He has managed very well on a small budget and if he feels the time is right for him to go, we understand that."

Brian could hold his head high. He had taken over at the club in the 2002-03 season after the resignation of Alan Shoulder following an embarrassing defeat in the FA Cup. The club were struggling near the foot of the table and Brian had steadied the ship and guided Bishop Auckland to promotion and to the Durham Challenge Cup final.

In 2003-04 the formation of the new Conference North and South was announced. The top 13 clubs would end up in the UniBond Premier League and from 14th downwards would go into the UniBond Division One. The club finished 13th and were promoted to the Premier League, although still three levels below the Football League which was their aspiration. The club would reach the semi-final of the League Cup and lose in the final of the Durham Challenge Cup.

In 2004-05 they were relegated on the last day of the season, and in 2005-06, after a disappointing start to the season and exit from the FA Cup, Brian decided enough was enough.

Bishops' Committee reluctantly accepted Brian Honour's resignation and invited applications for the vacancy.

However, that wasn't the end of Mr Honour's association with the famous amateur club.

In 2007 Brian was invited to return to the club. He got off to a great start with a 4-1 win over West Allotment. Bryan Stewart, Gavin Parkin, Darren Richardson and Ben Jackson were all on target for the Bishops, with Michael Fenwick replying.

So Brian was back at Bishops. The players were happy, the chairman was happy and Brian was happy ... well, for the time being anyway.

Horden Colliery Welfare

In the 2005-06 season Brian found himself coming back full circle to where his story started - at Horden Colliery, his birthplace.

The club was formed in 1908 as Horden Athletic and then in 1928, in the Wearside League, they became known as Horden Colliery Welfare.

In the Wearside League Horden won the League Championship on ten occasions, and in 1973 they achieved the treble - the League title, the Shipowner's Cup and the Monkwearmouth Cup.

They then moved on to the North Eastern League and Midland League before rejoining the Wearside League.

In 1975 Horden Colliery Welfare joined the Northern League and finished runners-up in 1980 and 1983. Then in 1984 they beat Blyth Spartans in the League Cup final.

Horden Colliery Welfare have a great tradition in the FA Cup.

In 1938-39 they reached the second round, narrowly going out to Football League opposition Newport County, 3-2. They also made it five times to the first round proper of the FA Cup. In 1948 they lost 1-0 to Southport, in 1952 they went down 2-1 to Accrington Stanley, in 1953 they were defeated by Wrexham 1-0, Scunthorpe beat them 1-0 the following year, and in 1981 the visitors Blackpool won 1-0 at Horden.

In 1985 Horden faced their biggest challenge in the club's history when they were relegated and Horden Colliery closed. The impact of the pit closure, the miners' strike and the loss of the team's main sponsor meant that for almost a decade the club would struggle. But in the late 1990s, under the management of Peter Todd and later Kevin Taylor, things started to look up.

Many famous players have been connected with Horden Colliery Welfare during their 100-year history: Bolton striker Bob Taylor; Stan Anderson, the only man to captain all three big north-east clubs; Colin Bell of Manchester City and England; Tommy Garrett of Blackpool; Ritchie Norman from Leicester City; Mick Fenton at York City; and of course Brian Honour of Hartlepool United.

After two seasons in which the club was unfortunate not to achieve promotion to the First Division, on Easter Monday 2003 they finally realised their ambition to compete in one of the most competitive Leagues in the country and Horden won the Durham County Challenge Cup.

Off the pitch the club has seen significant improvement, with new floodlights, a reopened social club, more hardstanding, new grandstand seats, a press box and a corporate hospitality area.

Chairman Norman Stephens is now in his fifth season with the club. His ambition and determination are truly infectious.

The refurbishment of the amenities under the grandstand are now complete, bringing the facilities into the twenty-first century. The changing rooms, showers, toilets, treatment room, referee's area, club shop and kitchen have all been rebuilt.

So what are Brian's recollections of his return to Horden?

"To be honest, it wasn't a happy time and I never realised my full potential," explained Brian. "It's a lovely club with smashing people, but it didn't work for me," he concluded sadly.

Brian now runs a successful school of football in the north-east. He is passing on his skills to the next generation of young players at schools and community centres in the area. He thoroughly enjoys his time at the various venues and who knows if Brian Honour will discover the next Paul Gascoigne playing on the fields of Durham.

It won't be for the want of trying, and as for the kids he teaches each week, well they idolise him.

Gary Walton Memorial - Charity Match

In September 2000 Brian appeared in charity match at Spennymoor. It would be one of many appearances that Brian would make to help people not so fortunate as himself.

The match was like something out of a 'Who's Who' of football, with the region's Football League clubs putting rivalry aside to help two little girls whose father, Gary Walton, had died in tragic circumstances outside the Miners Arms in his home village of Coundon, County Durham.

The Irish jump jockey, Christopher McGrath, was jailed for Gary's murder in 2001. 'Christy', as he known in the racing world, never denied he had got into a fight with Gary but he initially denied murder. When he appeared at the Crown Court at Teesside, on the advice of his barrister he entered a guilty plea and was jailed for life. Since the sentence, his family from Ireland, supported by almost 50 Members of Parliament, have been petitioning for an appeal.

Gary Walton was an extremely popular man in the village and his death was greeted with both anger and shock. He had been on the books of Newcastle United and was known locally as 'Hoss' after one of the Cartwright brothers in the popular television series *Bonanza*, which gives an indication as to his size and stature.

The game in which Brian played had been arranged by Alan Shoulder as part of a fund-raising effort to help Gary's widow, Susan, and their two children, Laura and Kara, at the time aged 11 and 8 respectively, who all attended the match. Peter Reid and Bryan Robson were also in attendance, and Kevin Keegan, the England manager, had sent a ball and a signed shirt to help raise funds.

The Sunderland/Middlesbrough team on the night included Jim Platt, Mark Proctor, Wayne Edgecumbe, Mick Horswill, Paul Atkinson, Gary Bennett, Paul Bracewell, Bryan Robson, Peter Reid, Adrian Heath, Terry Cochrane and the millionaire chairman of Middlesbrough, Steve Gibson.

The Newcastle team comprised Kevin Carr, John Carver, Mick Martin, Dave Barton, Peter Haddock, David McCreery, Chris Waddle, Archie Gourlay, Alan Shoulder, Micky Barker and, of course, Brian Honour.

The referee was Alan Wilkie and on the pitch the incidental details of the match show that Bryan Robson scored first for the combined Sunderland and Middlesbrough team. It was from an inch-perfect cross from Sunderland's assistant manager, Adrian Heath. Chris Waddle, who had travelled up from Sheffield, showed some of his old skills. Waddle had played with Gary Walton more than 20 years earlier at St James Park.

Robson, Cochrane, Wayne Edgecumbe (2) and Paul Atkinson scored for the Boro/Sunderland team and Andrew Sinclair and Brian Honour scored for Newcastle.

The final score was a 5-2 win to the red team, but the real winners of course were the children and widow of Gary Walton. However, in the end no amount of money can compensate for the loss of a father and husband.

Brian Honour and his footballing friends were only too pleased to help, and Brian would turn out many times in charitable matches long after his playing career ended through injury. Brian would also make appearances in the Northern Masters featured on Sky Television.

And Finally - What the Fans Think

Tim Girvan, Trimdon (www.timgirvan.co.uk):
"Well what can I say? Brian Honour epitomises everything I love about Pools: passion, determination and one of the original 'Never Say Die' Poolies.

"He gave 100% when playing for Pools. He was a winger, something you rarely see in the game nowadays. I remember him bombing down the right wing shrugging off challenges to get to the byeline and whip a perfect cross in.

"I remember true grit and determination and nothing more could be expected of a lad from the collieries, a 'Yakker', one of us. You could just tell every time he wore the Pools strip he was wanting to win every game, every challenge. He was and still is my favourite all-time Pools player. Once a Poolie always a Poolie."

Howard Jones, Owton Manor, Hartlepool:
"My recollection is of a derby match at Darlington. Can't remember the year. We had gone through on the train. The scores were level at 1-1 when up popped Brian to smash home a volley from fully 35 yards. He then ran over to where we were stood and dived full length into the Hartlepool fans. Brilliant!"

Paul 'Goffy' Gough (Goffymedia.com):
"Brian Honour … A True Pool Legend. Loved to see him dashing down the wing. My greatest memories would be that Promotion season when Cyril Knowles arrived at The Vic, seeing 'Jackie' flying down the touchline, attacking the town

end and being roared on by a packed Mill House was an awesome sight!"

Andy Wilson, Hartlepool Athletic Rugby FC:
"Brian played the last seven or eight games of the 2006/2007 season for Hartlepool Athletic Rugby FC. He was instrumental in that latter part of the season and helped to bring the young lads of the team on by improving their games. Not only was Brian a great player in his playing days, this showed when he played for the ATH as he always seemed to be two steps ahead of everyone else.

"Mark Gallagher our manager said that the older members of the team were a little star-struck, as they were now playing in the same team as their hero from when Brian played for Hartlepool United. Had it not been for Mark's brother Ian being a good friend of Brian's, these lads would probably not have been able to play in the same team as their idol."

"Brian was a true Poolie, one of my favourite players. I will always remember the goal he scored at Roker Park. And the one he scored at the Vic against Stockport I think, when he lobbed over the keeper from near the dugouts."
"Headlander".

A final word from Bob Moncur, Manager, Scotland and Newcastle United, the last man to lift a trophy at St James Park:
"Brian Honour was one of the first names on my team sheet when I managed Hartlepool United. He was committed, brave and skilful. He always gave 100%. Brian was a pleasure to work with and was a great competitor."

The message from all Hartlepool United fans to the wee man is simple:
thanks a million, Brian!

Postscript

In May 2008, at Hartlepool United's player of the year awards, Brian Honour received the player of the decade award for the 1990s. He also finished 3rd in the player of the century award behind winner Ritchie Humphreys and 1950s legend Wattie Moore.

Krimo

Hartlepool Marina will be the venue for the 2010 Tall Ships Race, when an estimated one million visitors will come to Hartlepool for the biggest sailing event in the Tall Ships calendar. In addition to the spectacle of seeing the old sailing ships enter the Marina, visitors can take in the Historic Quay, the Maritime Museum and the two resident ships, the Wingfield Castle and HMS Trincomalee. For a unique dining experience visitors will be able to dine at Krimo's, Portofino and Casa del Mar - part of the Krimo triangle on the Marina. Krimo's opened on 4th May 1985 with a mere £250 at the seaside resort of Seaton Carew (Hartlepool) in the north-east of England. The restaurant was put on the map with the help of immensely dedicated staff, a few of whom are still with us. From the very start, it was realised that Krimo's would be a runaway success because it was booked up weeks in advance due to the format of 'your table for the night'. At one time there wasn't a single free table on Saturdays for a whole 16 weeks. In July 1990, we moved out of the first-floor flat and doubled the seating. In April 2000, we opened the new Krimo's, our new self-designed 80-seater restaurant on Hartlepool Marina. Whilst retaining quite a few of the old menu's favourites, we have always encouraged the chefs to experiment with new dishes and, as a result, the menu now contains some exciting additions including, over the last two years, a few Algerian dishes, which have proved very popular. Krimo's has remained as popular as ever and, although we may now have the odd free table midweek, we still refuse people on Saturdays. The same format remains and so does the quality of ingredients. Krimo's has become a truly delightful oasis offering superb Mediterranean and Algerian cuisine in the idyllic setting of Hartlepool Marina. We have built this restaurant by listening to our customers and therefore your views and comments are greatly valued. Please take the time to send us an email with your comments and suggestions. Hartlepool Marina has brought a new breath of fresh air to the town. The Historic Quay, the replica of an 18th century port, was voted the best tourist attraction in 2000. HMS Trincomalee attracts thousands of visitors. In October 1998 Portofino was opened and its reputation has grown rapidly due to its beautifully prepared meals, mainly of Mediterranean style. Portofino places considerable emphasis on customer care and service, ensuring that the recipes are produced exactly as they should be by an energetic young team. Visitors to this happy bistro cannot help but be thrilled by the buzzing atmosphere created by the décor and carefully compiled music. The restaurant is situated in a pleasant setting overlooking the Historic Quay and Hartlepool Marina. Our latest addition to the Krimo 'triangle' is Casa del Mar, also on Hartlepool Marina, which offers more than 50 authentic tapas dishes. The common ingredient in all our restaurants is consistency.

www.krimos.co.uk
01429 266120
www.portofino.co.uk
01429 266166
www.casabar.co.uk
01429 222223

For all the latest news from Krimo, please log onto the blog at
www.krimosrestaurant.blogspot.com